TROUBLE-FREE
SWIMMING
POOLS

DAN RAMSEY

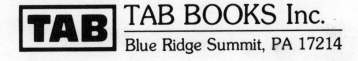
TAB BOOKS Inc.
Blue Ridge Summit, PA 17214

Other TAB Books by the Author

No. 1263 *How To Be A Disc Jockey*
No. 1458 *Building a Log Home from Scratch or Kit*
No. 1508 *The Complete Book of Fences*
No. 1568 *How to Forecast Weather*
No. 1578 *Doors, Windows and Skylights*
No. 1658 *Effective Lighting for Home and Business*
No. 1598 *Kerosene Heaters*
No. 1828 *Build Your Own Fitness Center*
No. 2339 *Student Pilot's Solo Practice Guide*

Dedicated to
Brendon Yun-Mo
who adopted us.

FIRST EDITION

FIRST PRINTING

Copyright © 1985 by TAB BOOKS Inc.

Printed in the United States of America

Library of Congress Cataloging in Publication Data

Ramsey, Dan, 1945-
Trouble-free swimming pools.

Includes index.
1. Swimming pools. I. Title.
TH4763.R34   1985   643'.55   85-4635
ISBN 0-8306-0808-7
ISBN 0-8306-1808-2 (pbk.)

Cover photograph courtesy of Sylvan Pools, photography by Berry & Homer
Photographics, Inc.

Contents

Acknowledgments

Many resources contributed to the completeness of this book including: National Spa and Pool Institute; Heldor Associates, Inc.; Richardson Industries, Inc.; Anchor Industries, Inc.; Doughboy Recreational, Inc.; Arneson Product, Inc.; Koppers Company, Inc.; Western Wood Products Association; California Redwood Association; Fabrico Manufacturing Corp.; Hytec, Inc.; Chem-Tab Chemical Corp.; Great Lakes Biochemical Co. Inc.; National Paint and Coatings Association, Inc.; Cover Pools, Inc.; Baja Industries, Inc.; Pool Technology Unlimited; U.S. Department of Agriculture; U.S. Department of Energy; Copper Development Association, Inc.; National Science Foundation; Brace Research Institute; and a special thanks to Scottie's Pool Sales and Clemmer's Spa and Hot Tubs of Vancouver, Washington.

Introduction

There are nearly 4.25 million swimming pools in the United States with a quarter million new units being installed each year—many by do-it-yourselfers with no prior skills.

Backyard pools offer a host of health, economic, and convenient benefits to their owners. Pools give parents the chance to share special experiences with their children. Older children are likely to spend more time at home when there's a pool around. Pool parties are an easy, casual way to entertain that lets you relax and enjoy the company of your guests. Swimming is good exercise that uses nearly all body muscles, increases blood circulation, and strengthens respiratory functions.

Trouble-Free Swimming Pools is comprehensively written for do-it-yourselfers, pool owners, pool contractors, and maintenance people with valuable information on in-ground, on-ground, and above-ground swimming pools from waders to large municipal indoor pools. This highly-illustrated title covers all aspects of swimming pool planning, excavation, construction, maintenance, safety, and enjoyment. There are also chapters on the solar pool and hot tubs and spas.

Trouble-Free Swimming Pools is written to help you plan, install, and enjoy your own swimming pool no matter where you live or what your budget.

Chapter 1

Pool Planning

How many times have you pictured yourself swimming early morning laps in your own backyard pool, wished the kids had a backyard playground where you could keep an eye on them, or even imagined parties around the pool on summer evenings? How many times have you thought about buying a pool but dismissed the idea because of the cost? Perhaps it's time to take another look at installing a backyard family pool center.

The cost is within the reach of many families. According to the National Spa and Pool Institute, more than half of the 250,000 people who buy pools each year earn less than $30,000 annually.

Amid economic turmoil and inflation, many families have rediscovered the joy of spending more of their leisure time at home. Pool ownership is an investment that pays off by making your home a more inviting place, adding to its resale value, and providing an alternative to a crowded beach, resort, or commercial pool.

YOUR OWN POOL

Whether you're part of the jet set or a middle-

class family, have flamboyant or conservative tastes, are an avid swimmer or just a sunbather, there's a pool for you. Innovations in pool construction and design have opened a whole new universe of aesthetic possibilities for an aquatic living center in which to play, exercise, and entertain.

A basic in-ground pool starts at $10,000. The final cost will depend on its size and the type of materials and landscaping required. Even if you live high atop a mountain or deep in a valley, have a small amount of space in which to build, or a limited budget, these obstacles can be overcome. An inexpensive above-ground pool starts at about $1,000.

Whatever your fantasy—a desert oasis, tropical paradise, Oriental garden, Spanish courtyard, or even a traditional ambience—you can create an aquatic environment that reflects your personality, life-style, and budget. This book will show you how to plan, install, decorate, and maintain a swimming pool no matter what your taste and budget.

One distinct trend in pool design is to add natural materials and elements that enhance the natural setting—stones, boulders, bricks, and wood

1

combined with a variety of colorful foliage to create the desired effect (Fig. 1-1). Often, they complement the materials used on the exterior of the house.

Pool designs today are versatile to handle a number of different activities, landscape problems, or custom-designed desires. Among the custom touches that create special effects and help retain the sun's warming rays are pool bottoms that are plastered in or painted in black or dark green. Dark colors absorb more heat, and the color gives the appearance of a lake or pond as it reflects surrounding trees, shrubs, and sky.

Challenging sites such as sloping backyards, difficult landscaping, or limited space shouldn't deter you from buying a pool. Cliff-hanging pools, kidney-shaped pools, above-ground pools, or custom-designed pools can suit your particular needs.

POOL SHAPES

How do you decide what pool is right for you? If you swim more than you entertain, you'll have different concerns than landlubbers. Pools can be custom-fitted to a lot in almost any shape you desire (Fig. 1-2). the choices are endless—rectangular, round, kidney shaped, square, freeform—and they come in all sizes. Modern options can satisfy every whim: spas, hot tubs, waterfalls, bridges, sliding

Fig. 1-1. Many of today's pools are built into natural settings. Courtesy NSPI.

Fig. 1-2. A pool can be any shape that fits your needs. Courtesy NSPI.

boards, gazebos, remote-control systems, and solar heating systems.

The most practical shapes are simple geometric figures that complement the lines of your home, won't compete with landscaping, and allow for creative use of the surrounding area. A rectangular pool (Fig. 1-3) is best for serious exercise. It's also the easiest and cheapest to build on a level site. An L-shaped pool is ideal because adults can swim laps in the long end while children can play and be taught to swim in the smaller part of the L.

An unusually shaped pool, like a zig zag, free-form, or octagon, may be the only way to save a tree or otherwise conform to the natural terrain. You can create your own fantasy island by building a free-form pool with a waterfall churning from an under-water ledge and a bridge crossing to the raised deck, spa, and firepit.

If you do a lot of swimming but are short on land, small pools are the answer. The long narrow shape of a lap pool is ideal for tight spaces or unusually sloped properties. The lap pool's smaller dimensions and water volume also reduce operating costs. It may measure 10 by 40 feet and range in depth from 3 to 5 feet.

Another option is a play pool with shallow depths of 3 1/2 feet at both ends. It's perfect for adults who want to play water basketball and

3

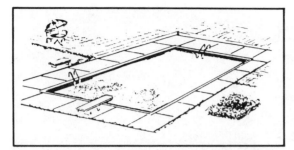

Fig. 1-3. Rectangular pool. Courtesy Polynesian Rectangle.

ed at moderate prices for playing water games like water polo and badminton.

If your family does a lot of outdoor entertaining, design a pool area that is picturesque (Fig. 1-4). Gazebos, sunscreens, cabanas, pool houses, and barbecue pits enhance the possibilities of creating a total outdoor living area. Have a barbeque on your patio deck. Use your pool house to dry off after a swim or to enjoy late-afternoon refreshments. Create a haven for solitude or an escape for your family and friends (Fig. 1-5).

volleyball at one end while children and toddlers play at the other. Swimmers can do their laps in between. Floats with baskets and nets can be purchas-

If your budget is flexible and you do a lot of entertaining, build an enclosed hospitality center. It allows you to dine and lounge without having to

Fig. 1-4. Pools can be designed for outdoor entertaining. Courtesy NSPI.

Fig. 1-5. Your pool can be a haven of rest and relaxation. Courtesy NSPI.

run in and out of the house to supply food and beverages to your family and poolside guests. Consider equipping your pool area with a guest house complete with kitchen. Or build a greenhouse to use as a pool house and dining room.

Even on a limited budget, the list of moderately priced extras is long: conventional heaters, solar panels, solar heat-retaining pool covers, automatic pool cleaners, slides, whirlpool spas, hot tubs, remote controllers, fencing, and pool landscaping.

CHOOSING A POOL TYPE

There are two basic types of pools from which

to choose: in-ground and above-ground. Prices vary dramatically and are determined by size, shape, materials, and landscaping required, and the difficulty of the site.

The most popularly priced type of in-ground pool, the vinyl-lined pool, is built with vinyl sides supported by a frame of aluminum, steel, plastic, masonry, block, or wood. It can be installed in less than a week and requires little maintenance.

Vinyl-lined pools come in predefined sizes and shapes. Once the pool is constructed, any tears in the liner can be repaired without draining the pool. Expect to replace the liner about once every 10 to

15 years at a cost of about $1,000. A typical 16-by-32-foot vinyl-lined pool sells for $10,000 to $12,000 complete with pump, filter, steps, ladders, surface skimmer, and minimal decking.

If you want an unusual pool configuration you might opt for the Gunite or air-sprayed concrete pool (Fig. 1-6). It's the most popular in-ground pool and is constructed of concrete sprayed on steel-reinforcing rods and finished with a fine coat of plaster. The Gunite pool's thick concrete shell helps it to withstand frost pressure in cooler climates, and it rarely requires structural repairs. Its prime advantage is that it can be custom-fitted to a lot in almost any shape you desire. Its price will depend on what part of the country you live in. A typical midsize Gunite pool costs $14,000, but could range between $10,600 and $18,000.

Your third option for an in-ground pool is fiberglass. Though limited in sizes and shapes, fiberglass can be less expensive than other in-ground pool types. A medium-sized fiberglass pool will cost between $8,000 and $16,000. Fiberglass is also easily maintained. Surface repairs aren't readily apparent, and algae is easily removed from the slippery material.

Complete information on in-ground pool excavation and construction will be covered in Chapters 2 and 3.

ABOVE-GROUND POOLS

If your budget can't stand the prices of in-ground pools, an above-ground pool (Fig. 1-7) can provide a refreshing place to swim and relax outside with your family.

For the simplest above-ground pool, you can

Fig. 1-6. Concrete pool. Courtesy NSPI.

Fig. 1-7. Typical above-ground pool. Courtesy NSPI.

buy a kit you put together yourself (Figs. 1-8 and 1-9) for as little as $300. Many pool buyers, however, want to make their pool more special by installing a deck around it and adding accessories (Figs. 1-10 through 1-14). In addition, most above-ground pools can be partially submerged or excavated into slop-

Fig. 1-8. Basic round above-ground pool. Courtesy Richardson Industries, Inc.

Fig. 1-9. Oval above-ground pool. Courtesy Richardson Industries, Inc.

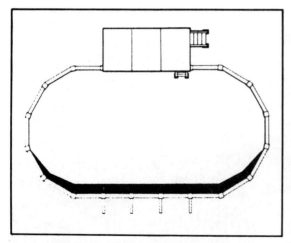

Fig. 1-10. Aerial view of small deck added to above-ground pool. Courtesy Richardson Industries, Inc.

Fig. 1-12. Fence and deck added to oval above-ground pool. Courtesy Richardson Industries, Inc.

ing ground, making them a more permanent and beautiful focus for your backyard. If you buy an above-ground pool and have it installed professionally, prices start at $1,000.

Chapter 4 will cover the selection and installation of above-ground swimming pools for the do-it-yourselfer.

PLANNING THE PERFECT POOL

When planning for a pool, decide how it's going to be used and what kind of surroundings you want.

A family of serious lap swimmers will need a water depth of at least 4 feet or more and a

minimum width of 6 feet. Divers must have a long, wide, and deep pool with water at least 7 1/2 feet deep and an overall pool size of approximately 16 by 30 feet. Allow 36 square feet of water for each swimmer and 100 square feet of water for each diver who will be sharing the pool with other swimmers.

If you play and entertain more than swim, opt for a pool with a large shallow area (usually 3 to 4 feet deep) in which to lounge and play. Don't skimp on deck space for sunbathing and socializing.

DECIDING ON A SHAPE

Standard rectangular, square, or kidney-shaped pools are the simplest shapes. They accommodate

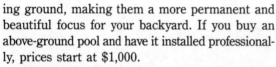

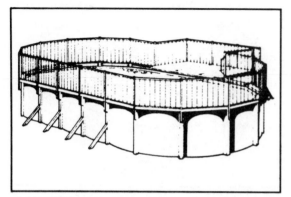

Fig. 1-11. Fence and deck around oval above-ground pool. Courtesy Richardson Industries, Inc.

Fig. 1-13. Larger deck added to larger oval pool. Courtesy Richardson Industries, Inc.

Fig. 1-14. A few trees and shrubs can add permanence to your above-ground pool. Courtesy Richardson Industries, Inc.

all types of swimming and won't compete for attention with your garden and trees.

What do you do if you live on a wedge-shaped lot, have less than an acre to spare, or go for the unconventional? A free-form pool weaving around the side of your house could save a grove of ash trees; a pool shaped like a musical note, seashell, or heart would leave nothing to the imagination about your personal interests. Since a custom pool is usually a one-of-a-kind item, it could be an attractive conversation piece (Figs. 1-15 through 1-18).

SITING YOUR POOL

The size of your lot, land contour, proximity to utility lines, equipment to be used by the pool contractor, and local building codes will all guide you in determining the approximate location of your pool (Fig. 1-19). Ideally, you'll have a panoramic view from inside to out, and the pool will be easily accessible. The pool will be in a sunny spot near the house, sheltered from prevailing winds, and away from large trees which shed leaves into the water.

Before you begin your pool plan, find the plot

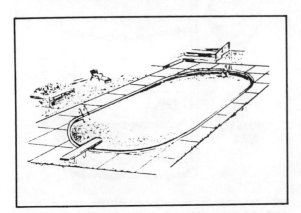

Fig. 1-15. The popular oval pool. Courtesy Polynesian Oval.

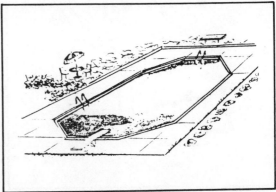

Fig. 1-16. The elongated octagon pool. Courtesy Polynesian Oblong.

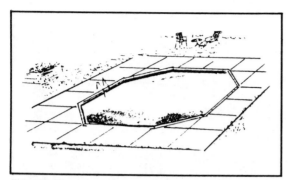

Fig. 1-17. The standard octagon pool. Courtesy Polynesian Octagon.

map you got with your property deed. This map will sometimes indicate if and where there are septic or fuel tanks buried in the ground which might be a hindrance to proper installation. The next step is to investigate all local requirements regarding swimming pools, such as building and electrical codes, regulations, ordinances, and building permits, and see that they are complied with. Your local gas, electric, telephone, and water companies will tell you of any buried cable and pipe.

Now, choose a nice sunny location and, using some stakes and string, stake-out your pool site and live with it for a few days. This will help you discover the perfect location by answering questions like:

☐ How accessible will other parts of the yard be?
☐ Will the pool be visible from frequently used rooms?
☐ Will the pool catch the afternoon sun when the pool is most frequently used?
☐ Where should walks and patio be placed?
☐ Can a slide or diving board be added?
☐ How about space for a lawn play area?

This is also the time to consider the location of the pool water filtration system. For maximum efficiency, the filter should be located no more than 25 feet from the pool with as few bends in the pipe as possible.

Avoid locating the pool in a low spot where the water table may be high. If the pool site is to be in a sloping area, try to arrange the pool so that the length, or long side of the pool, is parallel to the slope. For instance, if a pool is 20 by 40 feet and the ground slopes one inch per foot, set the 40-foot side parallel to the slope. The grade difference would then be 20 inches. If you set the short side

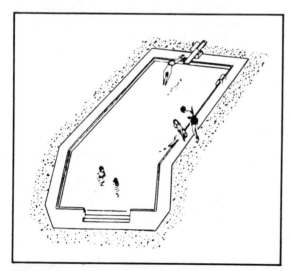

Fig. 1-18. You can modify the shape of your custom pool. Courtesy Heldor Associates, Inc.

Fig. 1-19. Placement or siting of your pool depends upon lot and home shapes. Courtesy NSPI.

parallel to the slope, the difference would be 40 inches.

EXTENDING YOUR POOL SEASON

You can extend the swimming season by six weeks or more in cooler climates and year-round in warmer climates by investing in a pool heater.

Compare the added expenses of a heater (equipment, cost, and installation), annual maintenance by an expert, escalating fuel costs, and additional uses of the pool before you decide. Your pool can be heated with gas, electricity, oil, or solar energy.

Gas is the most common and usually the cheapest and most efficient heating fuel. Electric heaters cost about the same to install as gas heaters. Oil-fired heaters are slightly more expensive than gas, but something to consider when natural gas isn't readily available in your area.

Letting the sun heat your pool can be a more cost-efficient heating method. An active solar system captures the sun's heat with solar collectors working with your existing pool pump to let water flow rapidly back into the pool. Its initial price and installation cost is about $4,000. That means it pays back in 10 to 15 years and makes you exempt from ever-rising fuel prices.

The simplest way to lower your heating costs is to cover your pool when it's not being used. A passive solar pool cover, which costs between $400 and $500, collects the sun's heat and reflects it back into the pool during the day and prevents heat loss during the night. It will pay for itself in energy savings in less than two years.

More detailed information on pool heating is offered in Chapter 6. Specific information on the solar pool is in Chapter 7.

POOL OPTIONS

Slides, diving boards, outdoor lighting, furniture, additional decking, and landscaping can make your pool more attractive and enjoyable. Conveniences such as automatic timers for heaters, pumps, domes, covers, liners, chemicals, and cleaning equipment can reduce maintenance time. Safety equipment such as a light, strong pole or strong rope will give you peace of mind.

Installing a fence around your pool is a good investment in safety and privacy. Most communities require a self-closing gate and fence tall enough to keep unsupervised small children, and for that matter, pets and nonswimmers out when you're not around. While you're swimming, a privacy fence discourages spectators and uninvited guests. The National Spa and Pool Institute recommends that the fence be at least 4 feet high. Additional information on planning and installing a fence around your pool is offered in my book *The Complete Book of Fences* (TAB Book No. 1508).

Though some options can be added to an existing pool, most accessories need to be incorporated into your initial pool design. You should talk to other pool owners and your pool contractor or retailer about which of these extras are most valuable. Along with taxes, utilities, and insurance, each will increase the price of your pool.

THE POOL CONTRACTOR

The selection of a pool company is as critical as the choice of an architect or contractor for a home. There are numerous pool contractors and retailers in business throughout the country—many with excellent reputations for honest dealings and a few with an eye for victims. One of the best ways of deciding which is which is to talk with other pool owners about their experiences and recommendations. Word-of-mouth advertising—pro or con—is usually the best.

Many reputable dealers and contractors are members of professional organizations, such as the National Spa and Pool Institute. The NSPI is a national association with numerous regional groups to support and police members in building reputable businesses.

Before having a pool installed, collect bids from two or three contractors and review estimates and contracts before signing. Also check with the Better Business Bureau in your area and verify the builder's references. Most contractors will be happy to supply the names of their previous customers. In states where contractor's licenses are required,

11

check with the State Contractor Licensing Board to be certain that the installing contractor is licensed, bonded, and insured for worker's compensation.

STRETCHING YOUR POOL DOLLAR

There are many things you can do to increase the value of your pool while you decrease its cost. Here are just a few to consider:

- ☐ Shop around for financing. Ask your builder for suggestions. In some cases the builder can handle the arrangements for you. In most cases it's better to finance through the lender who holds the mortgage on your home.
- ☐ Consider financing your pool by taking out a second trust loan on your house. Most banks and savings and loan associations will lend up to 80 percent of your home's market value, with a payback period of 15 or more years. Since the pool will add value to your property, it may give you the equity you need to qualify for a "second."
- ☐ Make sure the contract gives you maximum protection. Get itemized expenses for all materials and labor, including optional equipment, in writing.
- ☐ To insure the best bargaining position and possibly earn an automatic discount, have your pool installed off-season—midsummer to early fall.

DESIGNING YOUR POOL

Now that you understand the basic considerations and costs of owning a pool, let's design one for you that will fit your specific needs (Figs. 1-20 through 1-27).

By estimating the average number of people that will be using your pool, you can easily compute the needed size. As noted earlier, allow 36 square feet of surface per swimmer and 100 square feet per diver, minimum of one. For example, a party of ten swimmers (including two divers) would need 488 square feet of water surface—roughly a 16-by-30-foot pool. For a smaller pool with no divers

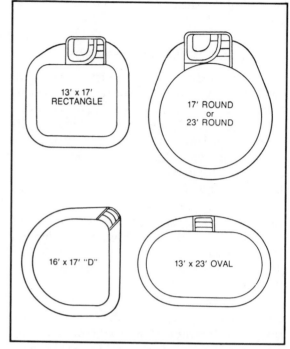

Fig. 1-20. Common pool shapes. Courtesy Pool Technology Unlimited.

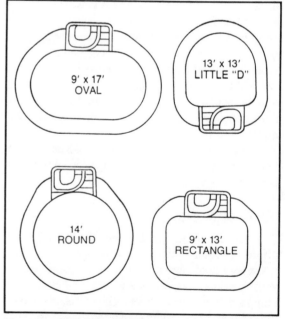

Fig. 1-21. Other common pool shapes. Courtesy Pool Technology Unlimited.

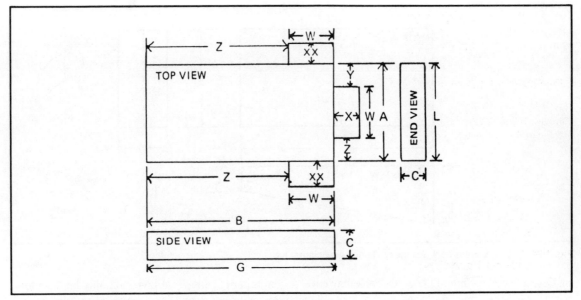

Fig. 1-22. Design of shallow pool. Courtesy Heldor Associates, Inc.

and an average of 5 swimmers, the surface should be estimated at 180 square feet—a 10-by-18-foot pool. Even so, an in-ground pool should be at least 15 by 30 feet, or 450 square feet of surface, for most homes.

The typical in-ground pool is between 15 by 30 feet (450 square feet) and 20 by 40 feet (800 square feet). Above-ground pools come in all sizes from waders up to 800 square feet of surface area.

Average pool depth should be between 3 1/2 and 4 feet at the shallow end to 8 feet at the deepest part—9 feet for competition diving.

The size and shape of your pool's deck will depend on many factors, including your budget, number of sunbathers, available space, pool shape, adjacent areas, and planned landscaping. For an above-ground pool the deck may simply be a 4-by-8-foot wooden deck at one side of the pool. For

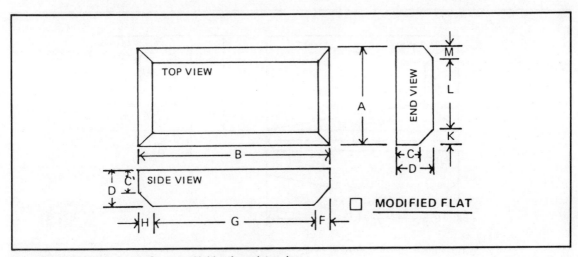

Fig. 1-23. Modified flat pool. Courtesy Heldor Associates, Inc.

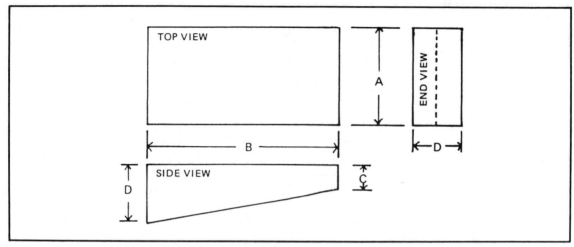

Fig. 1-24. Sloped bottom pool. Courtesy Heldor Associates, Inc.

an Olympic-size swimming pool the deck may cover a surface three times as large as the pool itself. Work with your plot map and illustrations throughout this book to decide on the most appropriate decking for your pool. Chapter 9 will cover this topic in greater detail.

LOCATING YOUR POOL

Earlier, we touched on the subject of deciding where to locate or place your pool. As you become more serious about this project you'll want to take a more informed look at the possibilities. There are

a number of considerations, including land contour, soil, wind, sun, and local building regulations.

The best place to locate your pool is on level ground. Sounds simple enough. The logic behind that statement is that level ground will allow you to excavate or clear the location easier, will make drainage problems simpler to handle, and will make decks, structures, and landscaping easier to solve. Much is going to be dictated by the "lay of the land," but the first rule of pool location is: site it on level ground if at all possible.

The type of soil around and under your pool will

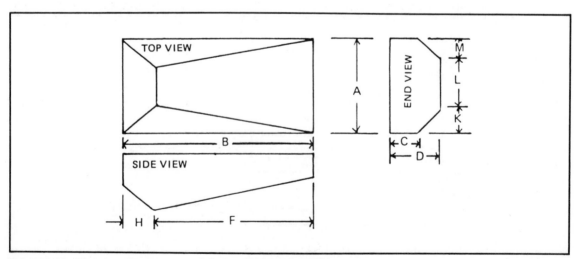

Fig. 1-25. Modified sloped bottom pool. Courtesy Heldor Associates, Inc.

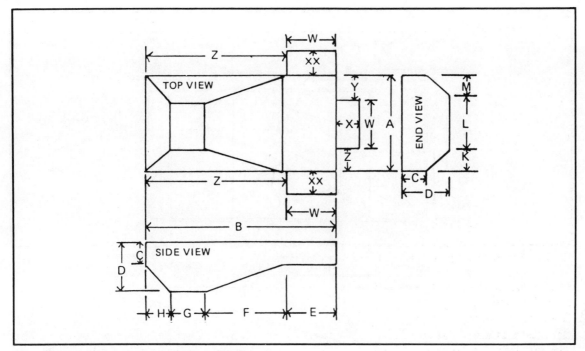

Fig. 1-26. Hopper pool. Courtesy Heldor Associates, Inc.

make a difference. The best soil is that which would support a healthy garden—firm, with a good balance of humus, aerated by sand and gravel. Rocks should be small and at a minimum. Soil samples can be tested by local laboratories or through the county extension service.

Minerals within the soil can also affect your pool. Some salts are highly corrosive to metal piping and fittings. Others may be tough on cast iron, but not steel. Have your soil tested for conductivity before installing your pool.

In some areas rock is the problem. An abundance of granite, shale, or gravel can cause numerous problems for the pool builder. On the plus side, once the hole is excavated in hard rock, you have an excellent pool foundation. Above-ground pools may be a more efficient investment for areas with rock problems.

Marshy soil is a problem in many areas. High-water tables can make drainage away from the pool site difficult. They can also make a concrete in-ground pool difficult to install. In one area of high-water tables, it was necessary to maintain water in

the pool at all times to insure that it would not pop out of the ground from water pressure below it.

By the same token, frozen soil can be a problem for pool builders. Excavation can only be done during certain months of the year. Pool shells must be thicker and stronger, and maintenance is more difficult. Most of these problems can be overcome, however, as long as the pool owner is willing to pay the price.

The sun is an important factor in the location and use of your swimming pool. The best location for your pool is near the house where it can be seen from inside at many locations. The house can cause shading problems, however, and reduce the amount of sun on bathers.

If possible, locate your pool on the south or west side of your home where the most amount of sun will shine. Break this rule if you are building your pool in an extremely hot part of the country where you want to reduce, but not eliminate, the sun's rays.

If you are planning to have a diving board, try to place it on the west side of the pool. This will put the strong afternoon sun at the diver's back

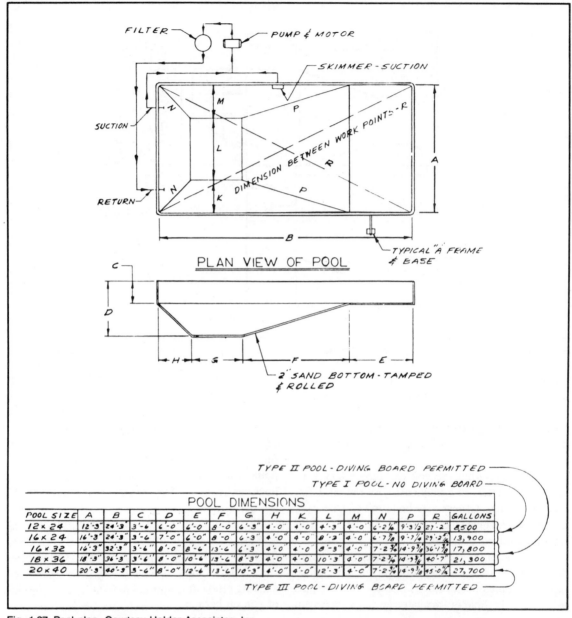

FILTER — PUMP & MOTOR

SKIMMER - SUCTION

SUCTION

RETURN

DIMENSION BETWEEN WORK POINTS - R

TYPICAL "A" FRAME
& BASE

A

B

PLAN VIEW OF POOL

C

D

H — G — F — E —

2" SAND BOTTOM - TAMPED
& ROLLED

TYPE II POOL - DIVING BOARD PERMITTED

TYPE I POOL - NO DIVING BOARD

POOL DIMENSIONS														
POOL SIZE	A	B	C	D	E	F	G	H	K	L	M	N	P	R	GALLONS
12 x 24	12'-3"	24'-3"	3'-6"	6'-0"	6'-0"	8'-0"	6'-3"	4'-0"	4'-0"	4'-3"	4'-0"	6'-2⅛"	9'-3½"	27'-2"	8,500
16 x 24	16'-3"	24'-3"	3'-6"	7'-0"	6'-0"	8'-0"	6'-3"	4'-0"	4'-0"	8'-3"	4'-0"	6'-7⅞"	9'-7¼"	29'-2¼"	13,900
16 x 32	16'-3"	32'-3"	3'-6"	8'-0"	8'-6"	13'-6"	6'-3"	4'-0"	4'-0"	8'-3"	4'-0"	7'-2¾"	14'-9⅜"	36'-1⅞"	17,800
18 x 36	18'-3"	36'-3"	3'-6"	8'-0"	10'-6"	13'-6"	8'-3"	4'-0"	4'-0"	10'-3"	4'-0"	7'-2¾"	14'-9⅜"	40'-7"	21,300
20 x 40	20'-3"	40'-3"	5'-6"	8'-0"	12'-6"	13'-6"	10'-3"	4'-0"	4'-0"	12'-3"	4'-0"	7'-2¾"	14'-9⅜"	45'-0⅛"	27,700

TYPE III POOL - DIVING BOARD PERMITTED

Fig. 1-27. Pool plan. Courtesy Heldor Associates, Inc.

rather than in his face. Following the same logic, build the sunning deck at the east side of the pool where sunbathers can enjoy the view of the pool while gathering solar rays.

As you locate your pool, consider that some people will not want to be in the direct sun. Set aside a shade area where natural or artificial shade can be offered near the pool.

The wind is another factor to be considered in planning and locating your pool. The wind can make life around the pool enjoyable—or miserable. Check prevailing winds in your area through observation

Fig. 1-28. Planning your pool by committee. Courtesy Doughboy Recreational, Inc.

or the National Weather Bureau. A flag set at your proposed pool site will tell much about winds. In fact, placing a number of small flags at various locations around your yard will help you decide the ideal site for your pool. It may be that a solid fence is cutting off the wind to your proposed pool site. Or a landscaped area is diverting the wind aside.

The ideal wind condition would be to have the wind blow away from your patio and toward your pool's skimmer to direct surface materials into it. It would blow leaves away from the pool while cooling bathers.

Finally, your pool siting should consider current landscaping. If possible, keep relandscaping costs to a minimum to insure the greatest efficiency of your pool dollar. Removing trees can be an expensive and even dangerous project. So is installing trees. Lawns can be replanted and bushes moved with little problem, but larger landscaping projects should be kept to a minimum. If you are installing a pool at a new home, however, you can design your pool landscaping with an open mind and a creative flair.

Landscaping around pools and pool structures will be covered in greater detail, with specific recommendations, in Chapter 9.

MAKING THE DECISION

There are many factors to be considered in planning your pool (Fig. 1-28), including your own needs, pool shapes, pool types, locations, related structures, options, costs, and contractors. In the coming chapters you'll take a closer look at the elements of installing and maintaining pool systems. Read them before you decide which pool is best for you. Meanwhile, picture yourself swimming in your pool or soaking up the sun on a warm afternoon.

Chapter 2

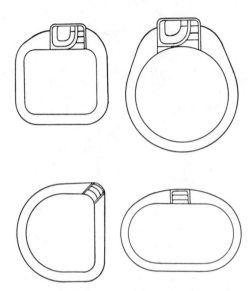

Pool Excavation

Whatever kind of in-ground pool you decide to install, its excavation is an important and costly part of construction. In this chapter you'll learn how to excavate a site for an in-ground pool (Fig. 2-1). This information is offered both for the do-it-yourselfer and the "sidewalk supervisor" who wants to deal more knowledgeably with the pool contractor.

The weight of the pool structure itself, plus the water it contains, must be carried ultimately by the ground. A soundly-excavated hole, which provides an even base for the pool to rest upon, will do much to prevent settling, possible cracks, and serious leaks.

As noted earlier, avoid extremely rocky soil; loose, sandy, or filled soil; and soil in which a high-water problem exists if at all possible. You can build your pool in locations with these conditions, but you will have extra problems and expense.

Rocky soil is not usually a problem for power excavating equipment, provided the rocks are not too big. If they are so large that they cannot be moved by a power shovel, they will have to be

blasted out—a job that calls for highly trained men.

If you don't want to blast out a huge rock, cropping, or underground ledge, you may be able to build an attractive pool around it. The rock will limit the shape and construction of the pool, however. Concrete or masonry would be logical choices in such a situation.

High-water or drainage problems will make it difficult for an excavating machine to move around and cut sharp walls because the soil will tend to sag. In some instances it may be necessary to bring in a pump to get rid of the water while the excavation work goes on. It might even have to operate while the pool structure is being completed.

It will also be difficult to make a clear-cut excavation if the soil is sandy. The walls will continue to slope. The deeper the excavation, the greater danger of cave-ins.

The nature of the soil often determines what kind of pool is best suited to it. Clearly defined excavations are not necessary for a concrete, masonry, steel, aluminum, or vinyl-lined pool. After these

Fig. 2-1. Pool excavation is an important and costly part of pool construction. Courtesy NSPI.

pools are erected, backfilling can take place. With backfilling, the excavation is made larger than the pool, and after it is installed, fill is placed around the walls. With Gunite, drypack, or fiberglass pools, however, the excavation must conform exactly to the size and shape of the pool.

POOL CONSTRUCTION METHODS

In a Gunite pool, concrete is sprayed directly against the soil. For this reason, an excavation must be made to the exact size of the pool (Fig. 2-2). The same is true of fiberglass pools. The fiberglass consists of a thin sheet which depends upon the earth at the sides and the bottom for its main support.

In removing dirt for concrete, masonry, vinyl-lined, or other pools which don't need an exact excavation, you can cut the hole about 2 feet wider on each side than the actual dimensions of the completed pool. This extra space will give workers the room they need to work in. For instance, if the size of the actual pool is to be 16 by 32 feet, the size of the hole should be about 20 by 36 feet.

EXCAVATING EQUIPMENT

If you plan to build a below-grade pool yourself, it will usually be worthwhile to hire a professional excavator. You could excavate by hand, of course, but it would cost hundreds of hours in time. Professional excavators have the equipment and experience to dig faster and more efficiently than manual labor.

In hiring an excavator, consider two factors: price and equipment. Some contractors rent shovels and bulldozers with an operator by the day. Call around and compare rates that may vary. First make sure that the operator has experience with pool excavation, especially if you're installing an exact-excavation pool. A normal pool can be excavated in one day. Another day may be needed for backfilling and regrading. You may also need to hire a dump truck to remove excess soil.

Almost any kind of equipment will be satisfactory if the hole doesn't have to be dug to exact specifications. Many contractors use a backhoe with a minimum capacity of a half-cubic yard for this type of work. This equipment can load excessive soil in-

Fig. 2-2. Concrete pool excavation must be made to the exact size of the pool. Courtesy NSPI.

to a truck and excavate a hole required for a hopper.

In digging for Gunite and fiberglass pools, a front-end loader is often used. The loader cuts away all but about 6 inches of the wall. The remaining 6 inches is precision-cut by hand. Usually the loader and hand-trimmers work together. The people working with shovels can throw their dirt where it will be picked up and carried off by machine.

One problem faced in this type of excavation is how to get the loader out of the hole without excessively cutting the walls. Some excavators start working at the deep end and move out at the shallow end. In this way, they disturb only a small section of the wall. The wall which the loader must break down in climbing out is then built up with sand bags, sometimes bonded together with cement. The Gunite is sprayed against this wall later.

TOOLS AND MATERIALS

The most popular do-it-yourself in-ground pool today is the vinyl-lined pool. It is constructed with steel or aluminum panels that are bolted together and covered with seamed vinyl sheets. Let's look at the tools and materials you will need for this project.

First, you will need a tractor-type backhoe with a minimum 14-foot reach or a Gradall to dig the pool excavation (Fig. 2-3). You'll also need shovels (Fig. 2-4), rakes (Fig. 2-5), picks, tamps, and related hand

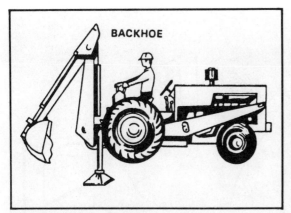

Fig. 2-3. Tractor-type backhoe or Gradall. Courtesy Heldor Associates, Inc.

Fig. 2-5. Rakes can be useful in grading pool bottoms. Courtesy Heldor Associates, Inc.

tools for those working at the site. These tools will primarily be used for finish work, such as adjustment of the hopper, hole, and final hand-trimming. A wooden or steel hand trowel will also be useful for smoothing sand or aggregate on the pool bottom (Fig. 2-6). Hand tampers and a garden roller can be used to compact sand at the bottom of the excavated hole.

Other necessary tools include a 6-foot folding rule, a 3-foot yardstick, and a 100-foot steel measuring tape for measuring the pool size and grade (Fig. 2-7). Other hand tools include a ratchet wrench with 9/16-inch and 1/2-inch sockets, 9/16-inch and 1/2-inch open-end wrenches for bolting panels (Fig. 2-8), and an 18-inch pipe wrench for installing the skimmer and filter fittings. You will need at least one medium and one large blade and Phillips-head

screw driver (Fig. 2-9). A pointed awl, a utility knife (Fig. 2-10), and a level (Fig. 2-11) will be useful in installing walls. Assorted pliers should also be on hand.

In addition, you will need a bag of lime, mason's chalk, or diatomaceous earth to lay out the pool shape and washed plaster sand for the pool bottom. A couple of canister vacuum cleaners or an industrial vacuum will also be helpful in cleaning up.

Fig. 2-4. Shovel and roller for pool excavation. Courtesy Heldor Associates, Inc.

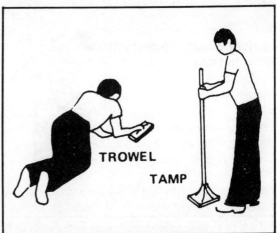

Fig. 2-6. Trowel and tamp. Courtesy Heldor Associates, Inc.

21

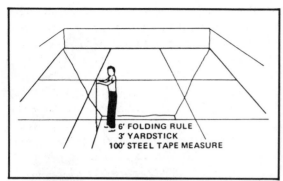

Fig. 2-7. Yardstick and measuring devices. Courtesy Heldor Associates, Inc.

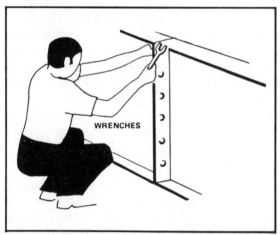

Fig. 2-8. Wrenches are used to install steel pool walls and other equipment. Courtesy Heldor Associates, Inc.

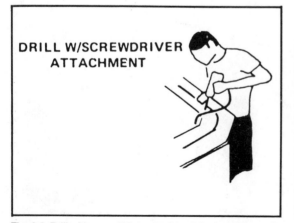

Fig. 2-9. Drill with screwdriver attachment for installing walls and other components. Courtesy Heldor Associates, Inc.

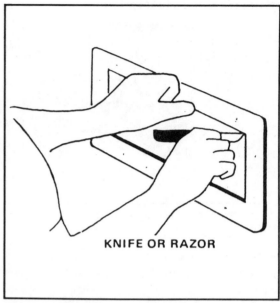

Fig. 2-10. Utility knife is useful for cutting vinyl. Courtesy Heldor Associates, Inc.

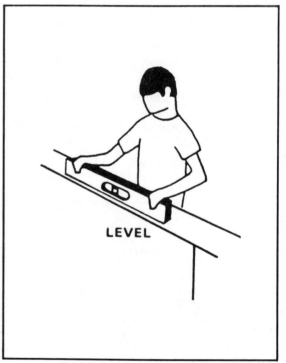

Fig. 2-11. A carpenter's level is used to check that the pool walls and other surfaces are level. Courtesy Heldor Associates, Inc.

ESTIMATING EXCAVATION

How much earth will you be moving as you excavate for your pool? Much depends upon the type and actual depth of the pool; however, here are some guidelines:

☐ Excavating the typical 16-by-24-foot pool will require the moving of about 10 1/2 tons of earth.

☐ For an average 16-by-32-foot pool you can estimate moving 13 tons of earth.

☐ The 18-by-36-foot pool will require the moving of about 14 tons of earth.

☐ The large 20-by-40-foot swimming pool will need an excavation of 15 tons of earth.

POOL LAYOUT

The most important part of your pool installation is proper layout and excavation. A great deal of time and effort will be saved if extra care is taken in this phase of the installation. Your pool dealer can perform this operation or can recommend a qualified contractor to lay out and excavate the pool site. Or you can do it yourself.

The outer dimensions of the pool site are to be 48 inches greater (24 inches on each side) than the actual pool size in order to provide working space when the pool walls are set in place. Specifically, this means a 16-foot-3-inch-by-32-foot-3-inch pool is excavated to 20 feet 3 inches by 36 feet 3 inches. (The pool is measured 3 inches oversize because of the corner radius.) Four stakes, one at each corner, are used to outline the perimeter of the excavation. Stakes should be 2 by 2s, or you may use the 1/2-inch round by 18-inch long staking rods included in many pool kits.

Try to allow some room around the pool for piling the backfill. Place the first stake at a point from which all measurements will begin. Using a building, fence or property line as a reference point, set the first two stakes as shown in Fig. 2-12 (stakes A and B). Set the remaining stakes (C and D) at the proper distances, according to the excavation layout chart.

The next step is to square the stakes so that a perfect rectangle is formed. This is accomplished by string lines 5 and 6 (Fig. 2-13). When line 5 is equal in length to line 6, the layout is square. Make

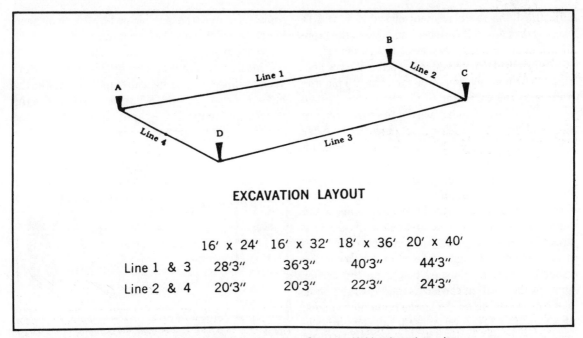

EXCAVATION LAYOUT

	16' x 24'	16' x 32'	18' x 36'	20' x 40'
Line 1 & 3	28'3"	36'3"	40'3"	44'3"
Line 2 & 4	20'3"	20'3"	22'3"	24'3"

Fig. 2-12. Typical pool excavation layout with measurements. Courtesy Heldor Associates, Inc.

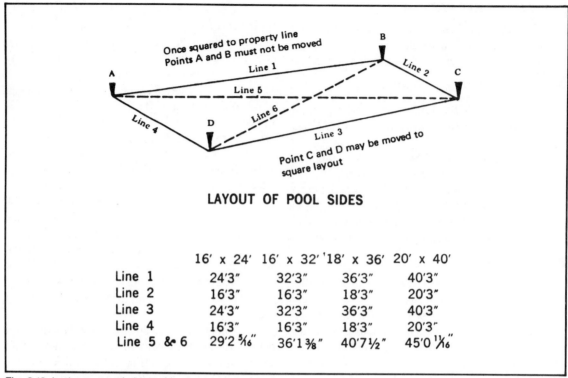

Once squared to property line
Points A and B must not be moved

A
B
C
D

Line 1
Line 2
Line 5
Line 4
Line 6
Line 3

Point C and D may be moved to
square layout

LAYOUT OF POOL SIDES

	16' x 24'	16' x 32'	18' x 36'	20' x 40'
Line 1	24'3"	32'3"	36'3"	40'3"
Line 2	16'3"	16'3"	18'3"	20'3"
Line 3	24'3"	32'3"	36'3"	40'3"
Line 4	16'3"	16'3"	18'3"	20'3"
Line 5 & 6	29'2 ⁵⁄₁₆"	36'1 ³⁄₈"	40'7½"	45'0 ¹⁄₁₆"

Fig. 2-13. Laying out pool sides with measurements. Courtesy Heldor Associates, Inc.

adjustments in the placement of stakes C and D. Since stakes A and B have been squared to the property line or building, they *must not* be moved.

When the layout is squared, outline the pool perimeter by pouring lime over the string. This line will guide the excavator.

A backhoe or Gradall will dig the most accurate hole and disturb the least amount of earth. After backfilling, any excess dirt can be easily loaded on a truck for removal.

Using a transit or dumpy level (Fig. 2-14), determine the elevations of each of the four corner posts. The finished pool level should be 6 inches above the high point and at least one foot below the existing ground to allow for grading and pitch away from the pool. The low point should be at least 1 foot in the ground. Mark the finished height on the corner stake at the position chosen as the top of the pool. Put corresponding marks on the remaining stakes. If a transit or line level is used, put it in a place where it will not be moved during excavation. If the transit is moved, the gin pole or 1-by-2-inch measuring stake will have to be remarked with new stake reference marks.

Mark your gin pole or 1-by-2-inch measuring stick at this level and measure up 36 inches at the highest corner. This 36-inch measurement plus the 6 inches above the highest ground point equals the

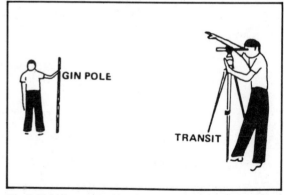

GIN POLE

TRANSIT

Fig. 2-14. Using a transit to determine corner post elevation. Courtesy Heldor Associates, Inc.

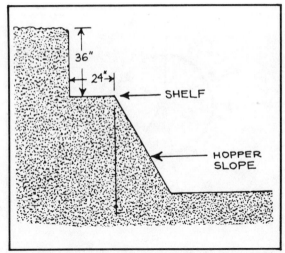

Fig. 2-15. Measuring the pool shelf. Courtesy Heldor Associates, Inc.

42-inch depth of the pool wall panel. Refer to Fig. 2-15. This mark at 36 inches will indicate to the excavator the depth of the dig, and give you the exact depth needed to level wall panels and the exact height of the top of the pool. The pool will be placed in the hole as the excavator digs.

As the excavation progresses, check constantly to be sure it remains level. A-frames should be located—one at every panel joining except corners—on your 2-foot shelf and a 1-by-1-foot square should be dug out for each A-frame by the

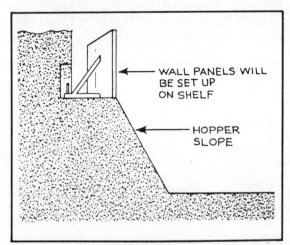

Fig. 2-16. Installing pool wall panels on shelf. Courtesy Heldor Associates, Inc.

excavator at this time (Fig. 2-16). The shelf on which the level panels will rest must be absolutely level, undisturbed earth.

Square the stakes as before, using lines 5 and 6. When line 5 is equal to line 6, the layout is squared. Make adjustments to stakes C and D. Don't move stakes A and B. After the layout is squared, run strings between the stakes and mark with lime as before.

EXCAVATING THE HOPPER

In order to have the excavator dig the most accurate hopper possible, it is important to give him guide marks by which he can gauge the depth and slope of the hopper as he digs (Fig. 2-17). The excavator should be helped as much as possible to get the bottom dimensions as perfect as possible. This will save hours of hand labor. The hopper bottom should be indicated by using lime guide marks on the working edge at the 36-inch level.

The excavated depth of the hopper should be about 3 to 4 inches deeper than the specified finish depth to compensate for the sand used for surfacing the bottom. Again your transit is employed to guide you to the proper depth. This is done by marking the gin pole or 1-by-2-inch stick to the proper depth. Proper excavation depth will be reached when the indicated mark on the gin pole or 1-by-2-inch pole is level with the horizontal mark in the transit site. Hand-trimming of the hopper slopes should be done before the excavator is finished so that a minimum amount of work will be required later.

A reminder: Sand can be ordered as soon as the excavator arrives, then piled nearby. About three

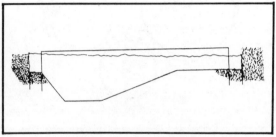

Fig. 2-17. Pool hopper. Courtesy Heldor Associates, Inc.

hours of hand shoveling can be saved if the hole is well raked and the excavator can put half the sand load in the hole with his machine.

It is important that a level foundation of undisturbed earth be provided at the 36-inch level for panel installation if you're building a vinyl-lined pool. Also it must be level where the A-frame base plates will be placed. A-frames are to be placed at each panel joint, except in the corners, as previously mentioned.

EXCAVATING THE KIDNEY POOL

Most swimming pools installed in-ground are of a rectangular or L-shape with straight sides and 90-degree corners. Many pools are built in radius shapes such as ovals, circles, and kidneys. Of these, the kidney is the most difficult, so let's use it as an example.

Visualize the construction of the kidney shape as a combination of intersecting circles (Fig. 2-18). If landscape allows, this is the most direct layout method. When the pool will be located near the house, however, access to a central or control point is eliminated. The following procedures describe locating the control point in a limited space situation (3) by using swing points 1 and 2 as starting points.

Before you begin, look at Fig. 2-19 for a bird's-eye view of the layout as it will appear with stakes. Two steel tapes should be used to find intersecting

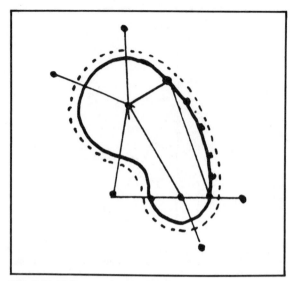

Fig. 2-19. Kidney pool stake layout.

points and swing arcs. String lines and chalk lines tend to stretch. You'll require about 15 2-by-2-inch stakes with a nail at the top for string lines, lime or mason's chalk, and mason line. The outer dimensions of the pool are excavated 48 inches greater (24 inches on each side) for vinyl-lined, concrete, and similar pools. This is done to provide working space to set the pool walls in place.

Step 1—Swing Point 1. Determine the distance the wader end will be from the property line and from the house. Example: for a 22-by-41-foot kidney pool that is to be 10 feet from the line and 10 feet from the house, see Fig. 2-20.

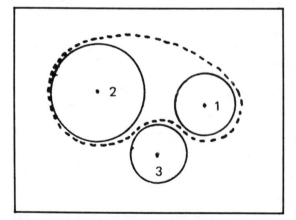

Fig. 2-18. Drawing the kidney-shaped pool. Courtesy Heldor Associates, Inc.

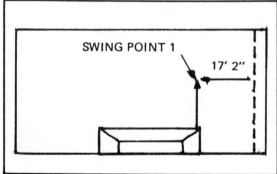

Fig. 2-20. Determining swing point 1. Courtesy Heldor Associates, Inc.

Remember, excavation will be enlarged by 24 inches, and if stairs are part of the pool, add an extra 4 feet. Add the wader-end radius, 7 feet 2 inches, to 10 feet for a total of 17 feet 2 inches. With a steel tape, measure 17 feet 2 inches from both points and stake where the lines intersect.

Step 2—Swing Point 2. Determine the desired distance the deep end will be from the opposite property line and the house (Fig. 2-21). If the pool will not fit adequately, it will have to be angled within the property lines. The distance from the property line will determine the angle. Run a string line 23 feet 1 7/8 inches (for a 22-by-41-foot pool) from swing point 1 to the deep-end area. This time, add the deep-end radius—11 feet—to the property line distance. Stake swing point 2 where the tape measure intersects with the steel tape from point 1.

Step 3—Mark Out Deep and Wader Radiuses. In the example, the wader end is 14 feet 4 inches in diameter. Using a steel tape 7 feet 2 inches from swing point 1, swing a 7-foot-2-inch radius marking the ground with spray paint or lime bucket (Fig. 2-22). The deep end is 22 feet in diameter. Use a string 11 feet from swing point 2 and mark out the deep-end radius.

Step 4—Control Point. Using a steel tape, swing and mark a short arc 14 feet 4 inches from swing point 1 at about a 45-degree angle toward the center of the pool (Fig. 2-23). Next, swing and mark a short arc 18 feet 2 inches from swing point 2. Fix your control point stake at the intersection of the arcs.

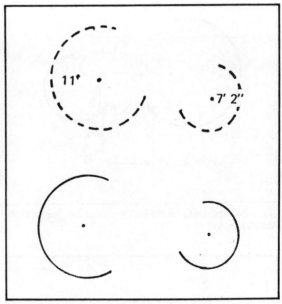

Fig. 2-22. Mark out deep and wader radiuses. Courtesy Heldor Associates, Inc.

Step 5—Inside Radius. Using a steel tape 7 feet 2 inches from the control point, swing and mark the inside radius (Fig. 2-24). The distance between points A and B (intersections of inside, wader-end and deep-end radiuses) must measure 10 feet 1 5/8 inches.

Step 6—Long Wall References. Drive a stake at the point of the intersection of a line 21 feet 6 inches from the control point to the wader radius (point C, Fig. 2-25). From point C, run a line 32 feet

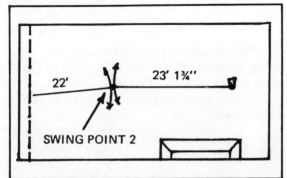

Fig. 2-21. Setting swing point 2. Courtesy Heldor Associates, Inc.

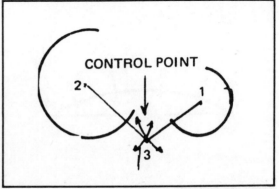

Fig. 2-23. Fixing the control point stake. Courtesy Heldor Associates, Inc.

27

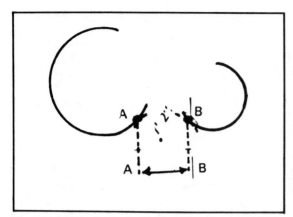

Fig. 2-24. Measuring for the inside radius. Courtesy Heldor Associates, Inc.

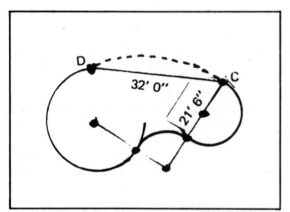

Fig. 2-25. Measuring for long wall references. Courtesy Heldor Associates, Inc.

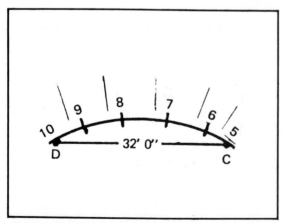

Fig. 2-26. Developing a long arc through a series of short arcs. Courtesy Heldor Associates, Inc.

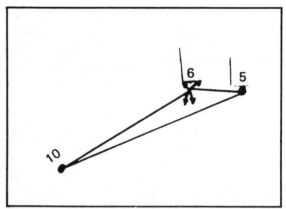

Fig. 2-27. Stake at the intersection of the arcs. Courtesy Heldor Associates, Inc.

to an intersecting point at the deep-end radius (point D).

Step 7—Swinging Long Wall Arc. The long wall arc is represented by panel joints 5 (wader end) through 10 (deep end). The long arc is accomplished through a series of short arcs swung from stakes C and D. Refer to Fig. 2-26. From joint 5 (C stake) swing a 6-foot-8 1/4-inch arc. From joint 10 (D stake), swing a 26-foot-3/8-inch arc. Stake at the intersection of the arcs (Fig. 2-27). Continue, following this formula:

22-by-41-foot pool		
5-6	=	6′ 8 1/4″
5-7	=	13′ 3 3/4″
10-9	=	6′ 8 1/4″
10-8	=	13′ 3 3/4″
10-6	=	26′ 0 3/8″
10-7	=	19′ 9 3/8″
5-9	=	26′ 0 3/8″
5-8	=	19′ 9 3/8″

When these four stakes have been fixed, run a string line from point C around them to point D and mark the arc with paint or lime.

Here are the measurements for an 18-by-34-foot kidney pool:

18-by-34-foot pool		
5-6	=	7′
5-7	=	13′ 10 3/8″
9-8	=	7′
9-7	=	13′ 10 3/8″

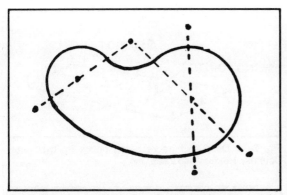

Fig. 2-28. Using a transit, fix reference stakes beyond the excavation. Courtesy Heldor Associates, Inc.

Step 8—Reference Stakes. Once the excavation is underway, all reference stakes except the control point will be lost to the shovel, the 24-inch overdig, and the backfill earth left poolside. Reestablishing these vital points can be done by either of two ways. The first is illustrated in Fig. 2-28. Using a transit, fix reference stakes 4 to 6 feet beyond the excavation. Then, by measuring between control and reference points, swing points can be reset. The second method is shown in Fig. 2-29. Measure two points outside of each radius. At the intersection of two steel tapes from each of the points, the swing points can be reestablished.

Step 9—Complete Layout. You can now refer to construction drawings (Fig. 2-30) for wader/deep-end break point, slope, and hopper dimension similar to those for rectangular pools.

EXCAVATING THE OVAL POOL

The oval-shaped swimming pool is also extremely popular as it offers the beauty of the kidney pool while allowing more straight water for lap swimming. Again, it is more difficult to lay out and excavate than the rectangular pool, but it can be done by the do-it-yourselfer who follows these simple directions.

Step 1—Primary Layout. Refer to Fig. 2-31. Stake out four lines representing the outside dimensions of your specific size and shape pool. Square the stakes as illustrated in Fig. 2-32. Then stake cross lines midpoint of both length and width (Fig. 2-33).

Step 2—Deep and Wader Swing Points. Specific swing points depend on the size and shape of your pool. Fix the wader swing point stake at the specified distance from stake F, along line 7 in Fig. 2-33. This is referred to as swing point 1 (Fig. 2-34). Follow the same procedure and stake the deep-end swing point 2.

Step 3—Mark Radiuses. Using a steel tape, swing the radius at both deep and wader ends. Mark the ground with spray paint or lime.

Step 4—Oval Long Wall Layout. Figure 2-35 illustrates the layout of a 17-by-32-foot oval pool long wall. The long wall swing point is located 26 feet 9 3/8 inches from stake G (past stake H). At the 26-foot-9 3/8-inch mark, and in line with stages G and H, fix swing point 3 stake. Swing and mark long wall radius.

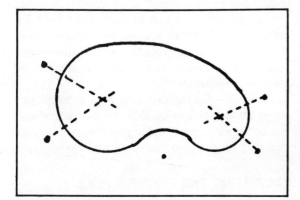

Fig. 2-29. Re-establish the swing points. Courtesy Heldor Associates, Inc.

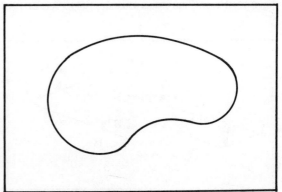

Fig. 2-30. Refer to construction drawings. Courtesy of Heldor Associates, Inc.

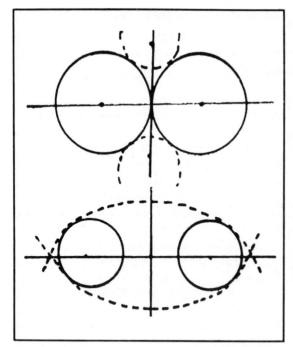

Fig. 2-31. Primary layout of oval swimming pool. Courtesy Heldor Associates, Inc.

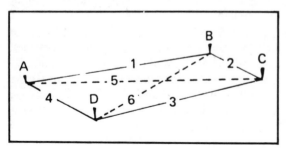

Fig. 2-32. Squaring the stakes. Courtesy Heldor Associates, Inc.

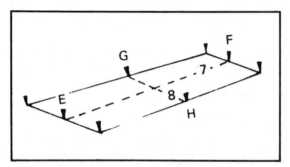

Fig. 2-33. Stake cross lines for length and width. Courtesy Heldor Associates, Inc.

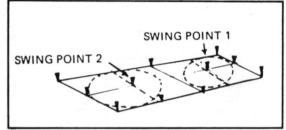

Fig. 2-34. Deep and wader swing points for oval pool. Courtesy Heldor Associates, Inc.

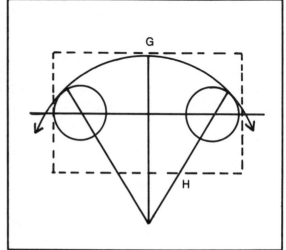

Fig. 2-35. Oval long wall layout. Courtesy Heldor Associates, Inc.

Step 5. Repeat Step 4 for the opposite wall. Fix swing point 4, 26 feet 9 3/8 inches from H stake (Fig. 2-36).

Step 6—Reference Stakes. See Step 8 for kidney pools. If you're building a vinyl-lined pool, the excavator must overdig the outside dimensions of the pool by 24 inches for a shelf which accommodates wall panels.

Step 7—Complete Layout. Refer to the construction drawing (Fig. 2-37) for the wader/deep-end break point, slope, and hopper dimensions. The excavator should also have a copy of the prints.

EXCAVATING THE FIGURE-8 POOL

Another popular swimming pool shape is the figure-8. Excavation and layout for this pool is

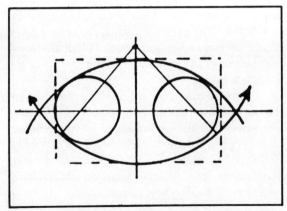

Fig. 2-36. Repeat layout on opposite wall. Courtesy Heldor Associates, Inc.

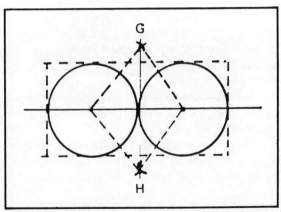

Fig. 2-39. Inside radius swing points. Courtesy Heldor Associates, Inc.

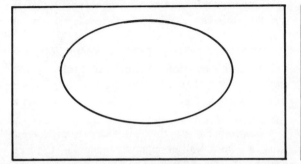

Fig. 2-37. Construction drawing for oval swimming pool. Courtesy Heldor Associates, Inc.

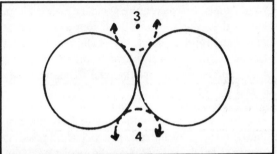

Fig. 2-40. Swing points 3 and 4. Courtesy Heldor Associates, Inc.

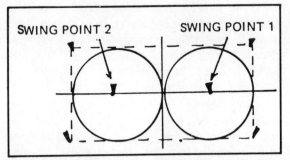

Fig. 2-38. Figure-8 pool swing points for radiuses. Courtesy Heldor Associates, Inc.

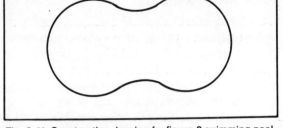

Fig. 2-41. Construction drawing for figure-8 swimming pool. Courtesy Heldor Associates, Inc.

similar to that of the oval pool. In fact, the first three steps are identical. Refer to Oval Pool Steps 1 through 3, then:

Step 4—Mark Radiuses. As illustrated in Fig. 2-38, swing and mark wader-end and deep-end radiuses using steel tape and spray paint or lime.

Your construction drawing will show the pool dimensions.

Step 5—Inside Radius Swing Points. Extend line 8 about 6 feet beyond, but in line with, stakes G and H. At the point where steel tapes, from swing points 1 and 2, intersect line 8 (Fig. 2-39), fix inside radius swing point 3. Swing and mark radius according to dimension specified in construction drawing. Establish swing point 4 for opposite wall and, in the same manner, swing and mark the inside radius (Fig. 2-40).

Step 6—Reference Stakes. Refer to Step 8 in excavating kidney pools, remembering to allow for overdigging shelf.

Step 7—Complete Layout. Refer to your construction drawing (Fig. 2-41) for wader/deep-end break point, slope, and hopper dimensions.

EXCAVATING FOR POURED CONCRETE

While excavating for a poured concrete swimming pool is not as critical as for other types of in-ground pools, it does require special consideration. Due to the weight of the pool, footings must be poured and reinforcement bar—called *rebar*—must also be installed. Otherwise the tremendous weight of the concrete may cause the pool structure to settle and crack.

As you excavate for a poured concrete swimming pool, remember that adequate room must be allowed on your lot for cement trucks and possibly a pumper truck to park near the pool site. If excavating during wet months, make sure that access ground is undisturbed so that heavy equipment can go in and out.

EXCAVATION SAFETY

When you are excavating your pool site, there are definite precautions that you should observe to prevent accidents. To avoid slides or cave-ins, the sides of excavations 4 feet or more in depth should be supported by substantial and adequate sheathing, sheet piling, bracing, or shoring. Otherwise, the sides should be sloped to the "angle of repose." The *angle of repose* is the angle, measured from the horizontal, of the natural slope of the side of a pile of sand poured through a funnel.

It is seldom practical to slope the sides of foundation and footing excavations to the angle of repose. Therefore, any excavation deeper than 4 feet should be braced. Why 4 feet? Because a person needs to be buried only to chest level to suffocate in a cave-in. The pressure against the chest makes breathing impossible and, even though the head may be out of the ground, a person can suffocate in such a cave-in.

There are numerous practical methods of vertical and horizontal sheathing installed for excavation safety. Sheathing consists of wooden planks, placed edge-to-edge, either horizontally or vertically. Horizontal planking is used for excavations with plane faces and vertical planking when it is necessary to follow curved faces.

GRADES

One aspect of pool excavation not mentioned is grading once the pool is constructed. Let's cover it briefly.

The term *grade* is used in several different senses in construction. In one sense it refers to the steepness of a slope. A slope, for example, which rises 3 vertical feet every 100 horizontal feet is a "3-percent grade."

In another sense, the term *grade* simply means surface. On a wall section, for example, the line which indicates the ground surface level outside the building or pool is marked "grade" or "grade line."

The elevation of a surface at a particular point is a *grade elevation*. A grade elevation may refer to an existing, natural earth surface or a stake used as a reference point, in which case the elevation is that of *existing guide*. It may also refer to a proposed surface to be created artificially and called *prescribed grade, plan grade,* or *finished grade*.

Grades should be considered in planning and excavating your pool site. For drainage, landscaping, and other purposes, the grade of your pool site may be changed from the "existing grade" to a new "finished grade." Make sure that the excavator is aware of this change before the swimming pool hole is dug. It can make a difference in the depth of the hole and the backfilling process when the pool is finally completed.

Chapter 3 will show you how to construct your excavated in-ground swimming pool.

Chapter 3

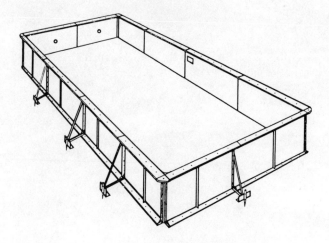

Pool Construction

The ol' swimmin' hole is dug! Now it's time to construct the pool walls and floor before filling it with water and swimmers.

Pool construction methods vary depending upon the type, size, and style of swimming pool you've decided to install. The construction of a Gunite pool is vastly different from that of a vinyl-lined pool. Each of the popular swimming pool types will be covered in this chapter.

POURED CONCRETE POOL CONSTRUCTION

The poured concrete pool (Fig. 3-1) is one of the most difficult to construct and is usually done by professional pool contractors. The do-it-yourselfer with concrete working experience may be able to construct or assist in the construction of the long-life concrete pool. The difficulty is not just in the pouring of concrete, but in the building and installation of pouring forms and the use of rebar.

The concrete wall for a pool is poured in much the same way as a house foundation. The *footings*, the base upon which the concrete wall resets, must

be laid on firm bearing soil. Otherwise the tremendous weight of the concrete may cause the pool structure to settle and crack.

For extra strength, vertical steel rods as well as horizontal steel bars should be used. The concrete is poured into the top of the form and is sometimes allowed to seep out the bottom so that it flows into the floor area and provides a continuous wall and floor—called a *monolithic shell*. The rest of the concrete for the floor is poured directly onto packed-down soil which has been covered with reinforcing steel.

The concrete should also be mixed with great care. The mix will be drier than that generally used in house foundations. A recommended ratio is 1 part cement to 2 1/2 parts of sand and 3 1/2 parts of gravel with 5 1/2 gallons of water per sack of cement. This mix has a stiff consistency which will provide a watertight wall and make it easier to shape the floor. Too much water would cause the concrete to run on a slope and make it difficult for the masons to trowel and float properly.

Fig. 3-1. Typical poured concrete pool. Courtesy NSPI.

Concrete walls should be plastered over to provide a surface that will not be abrasive when a swimmer comes in contact with it. This plaster is usually a blend of marble dust or silica sand with white cement, typically applied in two coats.

Concrete pools can also be painted without ever being plastered. They should be painted every one or two years. Instructions on painting your pool will be offered later. If painting is neglected, ugly splotches will appear on the floors and walls which can only be removed by sandblasting and repainting.

Concrete pools can either be very good or very bad. Much depends upon the workmanship. Another factor is the shape of the pool. A rectangular pool is normally easier to build than an odd-shaped pool which requires specialized forms

and journeyman skills in working with rebar and concrete forms.

GUNITE POOL CONSTRUCTION

Gunite is a concrete product that is sprayed into the excavation with special equipment. Instead of being poured into forms, the concrete is shot into a steel rebar mesh which lines the excavation. Because of the special equipment and skills needed to satisfactorily apply Gunite, it is normally not used by the do-it-yourselfer. An understanding of Gunite pool (Fig. 3-2) construction, however, will help you get your money's worth.

Since the form for the Gunite is made by the excavation, the soil must be a type that stands by itself. That means it must be of a heavy clay consistency rather than sandy. A good Gunite pool depends upon good excavation. Frequently a front-end loader is used to remove the dirt. It starts at the deep end of the pool and gradually works its way to the shallow end so that it can disturb the smallest surface when leaving the excavation hole. The pool site is then hand-trimmed to the proper contour and form.

Next, an inch or two of crushed rock is spread on the floor of the pool to strengthen the concrete and improve drainage. Then the reinforcement bar or rebar is installed. The *rebar* is the skeleton on which the Gunite will be sprayed, so it must follow the contour of the pool exactly. These rods are usually placed so that they will be about 4 inches from the edge of the finished wall and 2 inches from

the surface nearest the dirt. This will give a Gunite wall of 6 inches or more.

Exact size and spacing of the rebar rods depends upon individual conditions. A 3/8-inch rod is often used, spaced from 6 to 12 inches apart. Where horizontal rods meet vertical rods, 18-gauge wire is used to hold joints together. Many of the rods are placed so that they will strengthen both the sides and the floor.

The application of Gunite is a difficult process requiring special skill. So even if you have done most of the work yourself thus far, let a professional apply the Gunite. The applicator or nozzle operator must make sure that he shoots Gunite behind the steel and applies it evenly so there are no weak spots or thin areas. He must also avoid costly waste.

Once the gun operator is finished, masons go

Fig. 3-2. Gunite pools are popular in many regions.

Fig. 3-3. Concrete block and brick pool.

to work smoothing the walls and floor. They clean out pipelines and fill low spots. Once done, the surface should cure for about a week before being painted or plastered.

Gunite pools are more popular in the Western States than they are on the East Coast. They are especially popular for constructing unusually shaped pools because the excavation becomes the form. They are also less expensive to install than concrete pools discussed earlier.

On the minus side, Gunite pools have a greater tendency to crack or have maintenance problems than poured concrete or other types of pools. And they are still more expensive to install than most vinyl-lined pools. They require specialized tools and equipment not available to most do-it-yourself pool installers.

CONCRETE BLOCK POOL CONSTRUCTION

Building the walls of your pool out of concrete blocks is a method much more practical for the do-it-yourselfers (Fig. 3-3). The blocks can be placed one at a time with no specific time limit. You can start blocking one weekend and continue the next, finishing a month or two later if needed. Also, laying concrete block requires only minimal skill, and mistakes can be easily corrected.

Building a concrete block container for water is like building a house foundation. After the excavation is completed, a solid footing of poured concrete is required for the walls. The footing should be as wide as the blocks plus 4 to 6 inches on each side and should be 8 inches thick. For example, with 12-inch blocks the foundation could be 20 to 24 inches wide.

The pool footing is laid out in stair fashion in steps of 8 inches each. The reason is that the bottom of the pool must be a smooth slope, while the building blocks used are 8 inches tall. This footing should be made of a thick concrete mix, such as 1 part water to 2 1/2 parts sand and 3 1/2 parts gravel.

Making tight joints is especially important in the construction of a concrete block pool. To do this, some builders prefer to lay the first course of block while the footing is still slightly wet and not completely set. Another way to insure tight joints is to place a 2 by 6 atop the freshly poured footing so that it forms a groove 6 inches wide and 2 inches deep. When the 2 by 6s are removed, mortar is placed in them and atop the footing to provide a better key. After the first course is laid, the space inside the blocks is filled with mortar.

Reinforcing steel rods of 1/2 to 5/8 inch thickness can be extended through the footings to the floor and the concrete blocks. This will help prevent cracks due to possible settling later. Horizontal bars are placed on top of each row of blocks and tied into the layer of grout which holds the blocks together. Good construction practice calls for two rods per course—about 4 inches from the opposite sides of the wall. Where one rod meets another, there is a 2-foot overlap, and the rods are tied together with 16-gauge wire.

Vertical rods 1/2 inch in diameter are inserted in every block so that each unit is tied into the structure as a whole. For extra strong construction, some builders use 3/8-inch rods centered 8 inches apart.

What would normally be the top course of block to bring the pool wall to the desired height is not laid. Instead, the wall is stopped 8 inches below what the finished height will be. Above the top course of blocks, 3-foot lengths of reinforcing rods project every foot or so. After all the blocks are firmly in place and the mortar has hardened, the rods are bent to run parallel to the surface around the pool. The coping for the pool wall is put in place, extending 3 or 4 feet from the inside of the wall to include the walk around the pool's perimeter. Concrete for the top 8 inches of the wall and for the surrounding walk is poured at the same time. In this way, the walk is tied in to the top of the wall. The top of the pool, in turn, is tied into the rest of the structure.

During construction, allowance must be made for inlet and outlet pipes, for a lighting system, and other supportive systems. You can also build the wall without allowing for the pipes, then cut the openings later. When the pipes are in place, you simply fill the holes in with mortar.

Once the concrete block walls are in place, the floor can be laid. Best results are achieved with reinforcing rods about 1/2 inch in diameter laid in the floor about 1 foot apart. The bars should be tied with wire to rods projecting from the footing. In this way, a strong mesh is achieved.

You should plan on pouring the entire floor all at one time. If the pool floor is large, it's probably best to have the concrete delivered to your site by a ready-mix truck. The floor should be about 6 inches thick and should be given a smooth, trowel finish.

When the pool's basic structure is completed, the walls should be plastered with a 1/2-inch coating of cement and sand to seal the joints between the blocks and any holes which have been made for pipes and other openings. You can then add a good waterproofing paint on this cement.

The advantage of a concrete block pool is that it can be built at a lower cost than most other types. The primary disadvantage is that the walls expand and contract more readily than other types, and hairline cracks are more common. One solution to cracking is installing a vinyl liner within your concrete block pool, as will be discussed later in this chapter.

FIBERGLASS POOL CONSTRUCTION

Fiberglass pools have become increasingly popular in the last two decades, averaging 12 percent of all pools nationwide—and over a third of all pools installed in some regions. They are transported and installed in either one-piece elements or three-piece or four-piece sections. Much depends upon the size and style of pool.

Fiberglass pools are usually prefabricated at the factory and transported by truck to the site. As mentioned in Chapter 2, the fiberglass pool hole must be excavated to the exact size and depth of the installed shell. The pool is lowered into the ground as a complete unit, or the pieces can be bolted together after individual sections are placed in the hole. Seams where the sections join are covered with a special tape, then glued to form a permanently watertight finish. After the shell is put into place, a band of concrete is laid on the lip of the fiberglass to form the edge of the pool.

A properly installed fiberglass pool can give you many years of carefree service. The advantage to this type of pool is that it can be installed quickly—with swimmers enjoying the water within a week of the first excavation scoop. Also, fiberglass surfaces are smooth and require no painting.

If you live in the Western or Mountain States, you may find fiberglass pools readily available and at prices competitive with concrete and Gunite pools.

VINYL-LINED POOL CONSTRUCTION

Even more popular today are the vinyl-lined pools (Fig. 3-4). They account for a third of all new pools installed nationally. In fact, in many areas vinyl liners are installed in more than two-thirds of all pools built. A vinyl liner can be used with a concrete, masonry, steel, aluminum, or wood framework. This remarkable plastic material covers the entire interior of the pool in a continuous sheet. It provides a smooth interior finish which can be easily cleaned with a smooth brush.

Because the vinyl is itself waterproof, it isn't necessary to take elaborate waterproofing measures in building the basic structure of the pool. There is virtually no danger that water will get through the vinyl liner and onto the surface of the structural material.

A vinyl liner eliminates all painting problems. Most manufacturers guarantee their liners for five

Fig. 3-4. Vinyl-lined pools are becoming increasingly popular throughout the country.

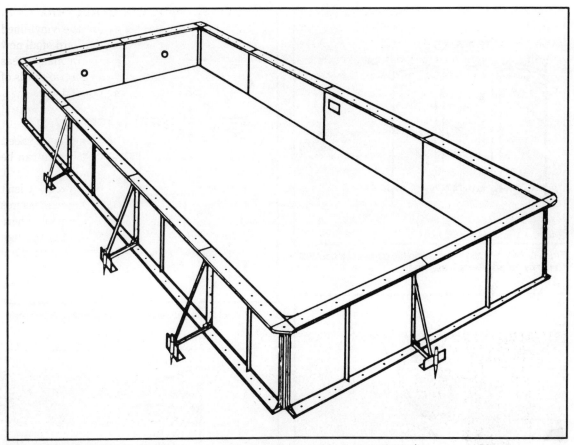

Fig. 3-5. Typical steel wall, vinyl-lined pool construction. Courtesy Heldor Associates, Inc.

years. Some have given trouble-free service for ten years and longer. If a liner develops holes through which water seeps and it must be replaced, it can be removed fairly easily. A new one can be substituted at an amortized cost nearly equal to the cost of regular repainting.

Installing a vinyl liner in a concrete pool is much the same as building a concrete pool. Only the final step is different: install the liner rather than plaster and paint the surface. Of course, the floor of a vinyl-lined pool consists of tamped-down sand or other pliable material instead of concrete.

Even more popular today is the erection of steel or aluminum walls which can be bolted into place and lined with a vinyl liner for an inexpensive and simple-to-build swimming pool in a short time. Figure 3-15 illustrates the construction of a typical

metal-walled, vinyl-lined pool. Figures 3-6 through 3-8 illustrate some of the components to such a pool. Take a moment to familiarize yourself with them, especially if you plan to construct such a pool.

Let's assume that your excavation is done with a 2-foot space between the wall and the outside excavation. Before the wall sections are lowered into the excavation, mark each panel along its entire length with a straight crayon line 2 inches from the bottom. Using typical 42-inch high panels, this line will measure the finished pool depth once the walls are in place. This line represents the finished height of the troweled, sand pool bottom. Refer to Fig. 3-9.

As the final hand-trimming of the excavation is being done, the wall panels are lowered onto the working border and leaned against the side of the excavation. Make a final check to see that the skim-

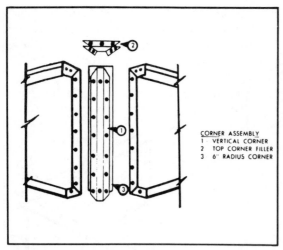

Fig. 3-6. Parts needed to assemble the corner of a pool wall.
Courtesy Heldor Associates, Inc.

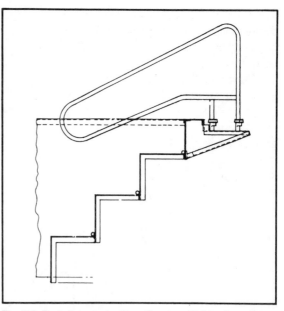

Fig. 3-8. Pool steps and railing. Courtesy Heldor Associates,
Inc.

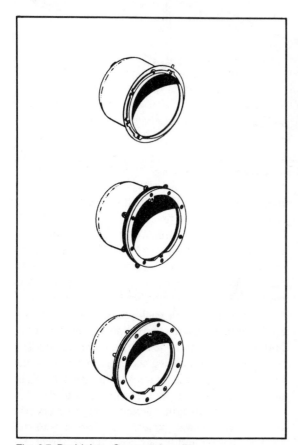

Fig. 3-7. Pool inlets. Courtesy Amerlite.

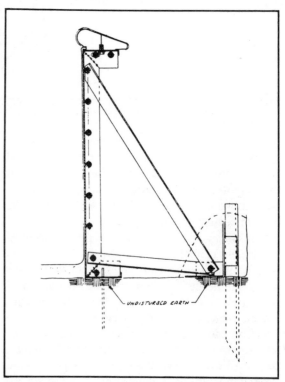

Fig. 3-9. Installing the pool wall. Courtesy Heldor Associates,
Inc.

mer panel and two outlet panels are placed in the desired location. After the panels have been properly placed in the excavation, the next step is to bolt them together.

Start bolting the panels together at one corner, using the excavation stakes as a reference mark. Working out from the corner in both directions will make the wall self-supporting as the assembly progresses around the pool. Take a sight through the transit as each panel is joined to insure that the pool level is maintained. Once square, the long wall parallel to the property line should not be moved.

Check each panel joint for level in relation to the first corner assembly. Be sure to install an anchoring A-frame at each panel joint. As each panel is leveled and inside surfaces are in line, bolts may be tightened. When the wall is completely assembled, the pool must be squared. This is accomplished by checking the diagonal measurements from the outside corners of the pool. When these two diagonal measurements are equal, drive a staking rod through the base of the panels near the corner. Next check the alignment of the bottom of the panels by using a string line. The straightness of this line can be maintained by staking a steel rod near each panel joint. Staking rods are driven down within 3 or 4 inches from the end.

Alignment of the top edge of the wall panels is accomplished by raising or lowering the A-frame base plates so that the walls will either tilt forward or back (in or out) as required. If the base plate needs to be raised, it should be shimmed with a non-compressible material such as a brick. *Do not* use dirt to shim. If the base plate needs to be lowered because the wall tilts inward, the ground under the plate should be carefully shaved away so the plate will reach the proper level.

When the base plates have been properly set, the pool wall will be plumb all around and the top edge will form a straight line from corner to corner. The drive stake should then be driven into the ground, through the slot in the base plate. Again, recheck the walls and corners for level, alignment, and squareness. If everything is satisfactory, stake-in the rest of the pool all around by driving in the steel rebar rods through the holes in the base of the

wall sections. This will hold the pool in position during the final phases of construction. Make certain that any voids under the wall sections, front and back, are filled.

Now that the wall sections are set, tape each wall joint with gray 2-inch duct tape. Taping joints will give the pool wall a smooth appearance. Install the ladder mount, skimmer, and skimmer support, then the diving board mount and deck supports if included. Once these mounts have been installed, concrete may be poured. If a main drain is used, make sure that this is installed first.

The A-frame base plates should now be concreted in place. It is recommended by many manufacturers that a concrete collar be poured around the entire base perimeter of the pool wall. This will set and secure every panel. Four yards of concrete is recommended for a 16-by-32-foot pool; 5 yards for an 18-by-36-foot pool, and 6 yards for a 20-by-40-foot swimming pool. Lesser amounts of concrete may be used, but the more you use the stronger the base of your pool will be.

Another important aspect of pool construction is the plumbing of a filtration and water system. Selection and installation of specific equipment will be covered in later chapters. Generally, you will run pipes straight down to virgin ground. If the concrete collar has already been poured, run the pipe to the top of the collar, using a thin layer of dirt on top to cushion the pipe. Make sure that if an automatic pool cleaner is planned, a return fitting is located at the center of the long wall closest to the filter system. This will be illustrated in Chapters 5 and 6.

INSTALLING POOL COPING

Coping is the edging around the pool that sits on the wall of your pool. Figures 3-10 and 3-11 illustrate common types of copings used in pool installations. Coping will either come with your pool kit or can be purchased separately through pool supply companies in your area.

As you install coping, don't tighten the bolts until all of the coping has been placed in position. Also, leave one section out until the bottom of your pool is finished. This will prevent coping from being

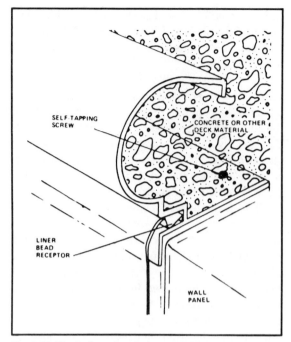

Fig. 3-10. Rim lock coping. Courtesy Heldor Associates, Inc.

damaged as you enter and exit the pool during bottom preparation. Leave about 1/8 inch of space between each length of coping. Special coping clips will cover this space.

Now align the coping so that it is straight and even around the entire pool. Tighten the bolts, but don't overtighten. A snug fit is all that is required. Next, place the coping clips over the space between the coping sections. If clips fit loosely, bend the nose of the clip slightly. Place the nose of the clip over the nose of the coping and hit the back of the clip. It should snap into place snugly.

There should be enough duct tape left to tape underneath the liner bead. This will make it easier to get good suction and vacuum air from between the liner and wall.

Install the extra piece of coping. You are now ready to prepare the pool bottom before installing the pool's vinyl liner.

POOL BOTTOM PREPARATION

Now that the walls are up, check the depth in various areas of the pool bottom and hopper in rela-

tion to the top of the wall. The pool floor should be very near its exact depth and only a small amount of hand-trimming will be necessary. The hopper depth may be 1 to 2 inches deeper than the specified dimension, but it should not be less than the dimension called for. You can check this by running a string line across the pool at the top of the walls and using a stick or folding rule to measure depth. The final surfacing of the pool bottom will determine the smoothness of the liner's finished appearance.

If a main drain is to be installed, a 2-by-2-by-1-foot deep area must be dug in the hopper bottom. This will be used to concrete-in the main drain. Pipe the side of the drain and run piping 3 inches below the surface of the side and under the wall panel. The drain should be 1 inch below the finished surface of the bottom to allow debris to run down the drain. Allow for 2 inches of sand over the concrete main drain pad.

Figure 3-12 illustrates how the pool's hopper should be finished. Sand or other material can be used to fill in the rough spots in the pool bottom and hopper so that the vinyl liner will be given a smooth base. Sand should be at least 2 inches deep. Wet the sand as needed so that it will stick to the hopper walls. The sand is shoveled from the bottom and worked upward. A wooden or steel pool trowel, available at larger hardware stores, is used to finish the surface of the sand.

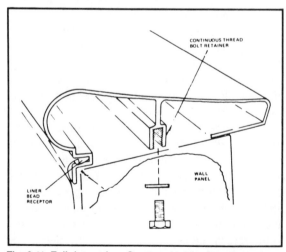

Fig. 3-11. Full rim coping. Courtesy Heldor Associates, Inc.

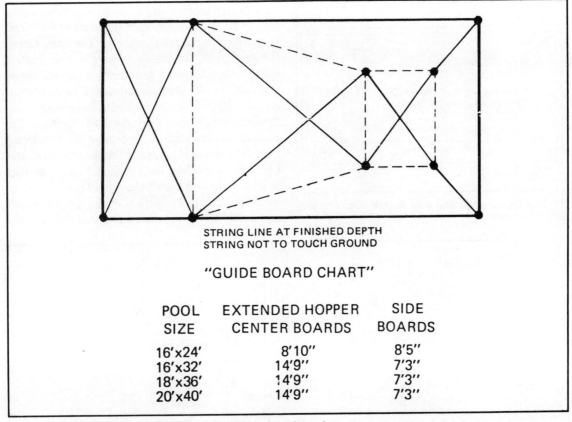

STRING LINE AT FINISHED DEPTH
STRING NOT TO TOUCH GROUND

"GUIDE BOARD CHART"

POOL SIZE	EXTENDED HOPPER CENTER BOARDS	SIDE BOARDS
16'x24'	8'10"	8'5"
16'x32'	14'9"	7'3"
18'x36'	14'9"	7'3"
20'x40'	14'9"	7'3"

Fig. 3-12. Finishing the pool hopper. Courtesy Heldor Associates, Inc.

When finished, the sand should be firm and smooth. This surface will determine the finished appearance of the pool bottom after the liner has been installed. If a pebble bottom liner is to be installed, a poorly troweled bottom will not be noticed. But all lines must be straight. Any particles of sand or dirt should be wiped from the wall surface, making certain that the walls are completely clean.

In some cases, it is most practical to install a hard bottom under your vinyl-lined swimming pool. A high water table or other condition could undermine the hopper and quickly destroy your hard work and expense. There are two popular hard bottom procedures. One is to mix the washed sand with dry cement (3:1), then wet the finished bottom using a very fine water spray and allow it to dry at least two hours before installing the liner. The second method uses vermiculite with the cement. Ask your pool supplier about this method and its requirements.

VINYL POOL LINER INSTALLATION

Vinyl liners are best installed in warm weather because the material is more pliable, can be handled better, and packing wrinkles will disappear more quickly. If the liner is to be installed in cool weather, store it in a heated room or basement for a day or two before installation.

Before the liner is unpacked, check the pool bottom once again for stones, twigs, or sharp objects and remove them. Wipe the walls clean. Install the skimmers and inlets, coping, and tape panel joints.

After the liner is unpacked, make sure that it is not dragged or damaged on any protruding object. Place the liner on the edge of the shallow end with arrows facing the pool (Fig. 3-13). Unfold the

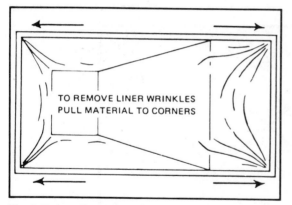

TO REMOVE LINER WRINKLES PULL MATERIAL TO CORNERS

Fig. 3-13. Installing the vinyl liner in your pool. Courtesy Heldor Associates, Inc.

liner to both sides, going to the pool corners. Carry the liner to the transition of the shallow and deep ends and rest the liner on the pool bottom. Grasp the corners of the exposed top flap. The liner is usually fan-folded and will unfold automatically as you walk it to the shallow-end wall. Line up bottom corners of the liner at the shallow end wall. Position and adjust the liner until all points in the shallow end are aligned. To prevent the positioned liner from moving, secure at the corners with sand bags or water tubes. Refer to Fig. 3-14 for instructions to help you install the vinyl liner.

Next, grasp the corners of the deep-end wall and unfold as you did the shallow end. In the same

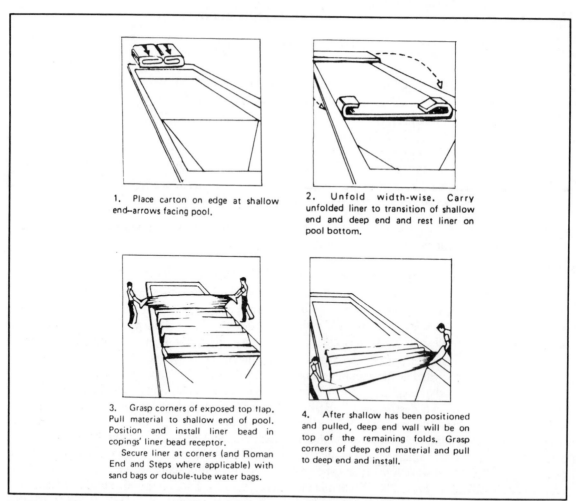

1. Place carton on edge at shallow end—arrows facing pool.

2. Unfold width-wise. Carry unfolded liner to transition of shallow end and deep end and rest liner on pool bottom.

3. Grasp corners of exposed top flap. Pull material to shallow end of pool. Position and install liner bead in copings' liner bead receptor.
   Secure liner at corners (and Roman End and Steps where applicable) with sand bags or double-tube water bags.

4. After shallow has been positioned and pulled, deep end wall will be on top of the remaining folds. Grasp corners of deep end material and pull to deep end and install.

Fig. 3-14. Step-by-step vinyl liner installation instructions. Courtesy Heldor Associates, Inc.

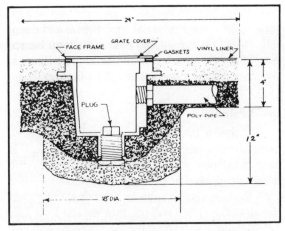

Fig. 3-15. Pool drain. Courtesy Heldor Associates, Inc.

Fig. 3-17. Aligning the pool drain plate. Courtesy Heldor Associates, Inc.

manner, position and align the deep end of the pool, eliminating any wrinkles by pulling and positioning the liner. When pulling the liner, always grasp a heavy fold of material with both hands. The heavy gauge of the vinyl will take a lot of pull without damage.

Make sure all corners are aligned perfectly and fit snugly. Once the liner is in position, the liner bead can be inserted into the bead receptor channel in the coping. Start to snap the bead into the coping. Snap in 1 1/2 feet on either side of each corner. After both shallow end corners are snapped in, proceed

to the deep end and repeat the procedure, making certain the bottom corner of the liner meets the bottom corner of the pool. When all corners have been snapped in, the center may be inserted to relieve the pressure.

Snap in the remaining material working toward the corners. When the liner bead has been completely inserted in the bead receptor, place the vacuum hose through the top of the skimmer, making sure all inlet and outlet openings are installed (Fig. 3-15 through 3-18). Start the vacuum. You will notice that the vacuum's suction will be helpful in removing

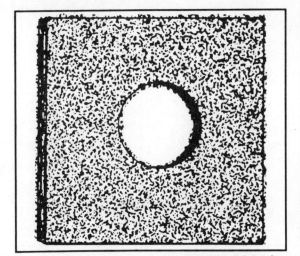

Fig. 3-16. Pool drain plate. Courtesy Heldor Associates, Inc.

Fig. 3-18. Installing the pool drain. Courtesy Heldor Associates, Inc.

45

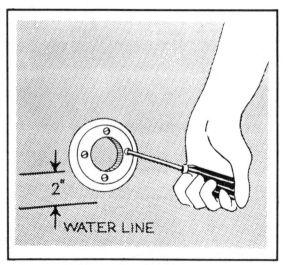

Fig. 3-19. Installing the inlet opening. Courtesy Heldor Associates, Inc.

reaches the base of the inlet, screw in the inlet face plate and cut liner material from the inlet opening (Fig. 3-19). *Do not* cut the liner opening until the plumbing is completely finished and the liner is stretched by the pool water.

BACKFILLING

At this point, backfilling should be started. Cover the concrete collar that surrounds the outside base of the pool with a thin layer of sand (about 6 inches deep) so that piping will not make contact with the concrete's rough surface. Installing your piping at this depth will put it below the frost line. Setting it atop sand on the concrete collar will prevent the stress caused by settling in an on-earth pipe installation.

The earth used for backfill should contain a minimum amount of clay and absolutely no shale or large rocks. The bottom layer of backfill should be a porous material to allow proper drainage away from the pool. Leftover sand is an excellent material. Backfill may be wetted or puddled when placed behind the wall sections to hasten settlement if a patio is to be installed within a few weeks after the pool installation. Maximum compaction of the backfill will be obtained if a tamping device is used.

Since the pool walls are self-supporting, it is not

wrinkles. All wrinkles should be removed before water is started into the pool.

With the vacuum running, start filling the pool with a garden hose. Lay the hose on the bottom and don't let it spray water making depressions in the bottom. Fill the pool no faster than you can remove wrinkles. Underwater wrinkles are impossible to remove, though they do not damage the liner.

Continue to fill the pool. When the water level

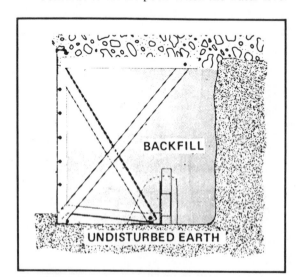

Fig. 3-20. Backfilling around your pool. Courtesy Heldor Associates, Inc.

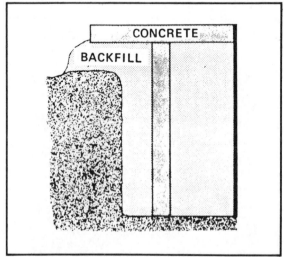

Fig. 3-21. Backfilling using a concrete retaining wall.

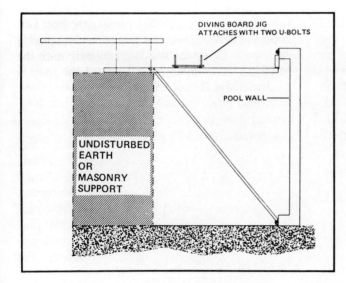

Fig. 3-22. Installing the diving board after backfilling.

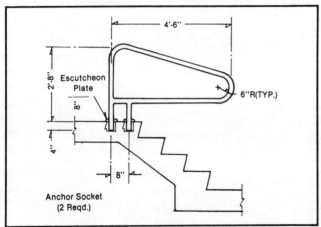

Fig. 3-23. Installing the pool entry rail.

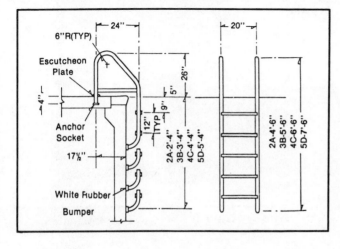

Fig. 3-24. Installing the pool entry ladder and rail.

absolutely necessary that the backfilling progress at the same rate that the water is rising up the walls.

It is a good idea to keep the earth, removed from the pool excavation, nearby. This earth will be needed to fill-in the void left by your 2-foot work shelf. With plumbing completed, and as the pool is being filled with water, you can begin to backfill as illustrated in Figs. 3-20 through 3-24. Slope the backfill away from the pool for good drainage. The slope will prevent excessive rain water from draining through the earth around the pool perimeter and possibly undermining the pool's sand bottom.

Installation of pool filters, heaters, skimmers, plumbing, strainers, and other equipment will be covered later. Let's take a look at the selection and installation of above-ground swimming pools.

Chapter 4

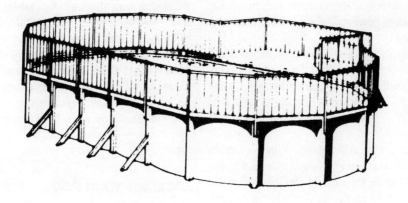

Above-Ground Pools

If your budget can't stand the prices of in-ground pools, an above-ground pool can provide a refreshing place to swim and relax outside with your family and friends.

For the simplest above-ground pool, you can buy a kit you put together yourself for as little as $300. Many pool buyers, however, want to make their pool more special by putting a deck around it and adding accessories. In addition, most above-ground pools can be partially submerged or excavated into sloping ground, making them a more permanent and beautiful focus for your backyard.

Economy is not the only consideration in installing an above-ground pool. Many homeowners and renters enjoy the benefits of a pool, but move too frequently to make below-ground pool installation practical or affordable. Above-ground pools can be packed up and moved in as little as one day.

One disadvantage to above-ground swimming pools is their depth. Unless special excavation is done, an above-ground swimming pool is limited to 4 feet in depth. This is no problem for family wading and swimming, but it is not deep enough for diving.

Above-ground swimming pools come in all sizes, shapes, designs, and price ranges. A backyard wading pool of a 5-foot diameter can be purchased for under $25. A regulation-size above-ground pool may cost $3,000 to $5,000 or more, depending upon amenities.

TYPES OF ABOVE-GROUND POOLS

While most any type of swimming pool can be built on or above the ground, the most popular are those assembled by the do-it-yourselfer rather than constructed by the pool contractor.

You may hear the term "on-ground pool" as opposed to "above-ground pool." What's the difference? *On-ground pools*, with few exceptions, are constructed of rigid wall panels that are attached successively to each other to produce a straight-sided rectangular or other geometrically shaped pool. On the other hand, above-ground pools are mostly constructed using a continuous flexible wall that best lends itself to round or oval shapes. These provide uniform distribution of forces from the water within the pool. The main structural feature is a continuous flexible wall member with inherent strength in the semicircular ends. It requires bracing or buttressing, however, on the straight or long sides of the oval.

Another distinction is the inclusion of full decking around on-ground pools. This construction feature lends itself more to on-ground pools. It then becomes a part of the external bracing system that serves to hold the straight walls in a vertical position.

There are other differences. Filter systems designed for above-ground pools are attached to the structure by flexible piping and flexible electrical hookups. On-ground pools, on the other hand, are generally identified by rigid piping and flexible electrical connections.

Both on-ground and above-ground pools are sold in kit form and are erected on the site. Because of the fewer parts and the greater ease of assembly, above-ground pools are generally in a more portable or storable form. In most cases, on-ground pools are not portable.

Popular above-ground pool sizes range from 12-foot rounds with a 3-foot depth (2,500 gallons) up to 16-by-40-foot ovals with a 4-foot depth (17,600 gallons). Rectangular pools range from 12-by-20-foot (7,200 gallons) to 20-by-40-foot (24,000 gallons) sizes. Octagon pools are also popular above-grounders.

Due to the many similarities between on-ground and above-ground pools, we will consider them together as above-ground pools.

INSTALLING YOUR ABOVE-GROUND POOL

By nature, an above-ground pool is simpler and less costly to install than an in-ground pool. The major reason is that excavation is eliminated. The walls, floor, and deck are all above ground level in most cases. Due to the kit form of above-ground pools, labor is saved as costly construction labor is not needed. The average homeowner can set up an above-ground pool in a few hours or a few days.

This chapter illustrates a *typical* above-ground pool installation. There will be differences between

sizes and manufacturers, but the concepts remain the same. The idea is to follow directions explicitly without taking shortcuts or making omissions. You want a wrinkle-free, level installation that is easy to maintain and enjoy for many seasons.

Figure 4-1 illustrates the tools you will probably need to install your above-ground pool. They include: a ball of heavy string, a tape measure, crayon or felt-tip pen, screwdriver, nails, 2-by-4-foot board of pool radius length, a carpenter's level, hammer, shovel, wooden stake, and a roll of masking tape.

LOCATING YOUR POOL

Choose firm, level ground for the site of your pool. Don't assemble your pool on concrete, loose sand, gravel, asphalt, tar paper, blacktop, or any oil-based materials, or on areas recently treated with oil-based weed killers or other chemicals. Also, avoid areas where nut grass or Bermuda grass grow. If grass is unavoidable, check with your local farm or garden supply for a suitable nonoil-based soil

Fig. 4-1. Tools used in installing above-ground pools. Courtesy Doughboy Recreational, Inc.

sterilant or herbicide. Be sure your pool area is free from stone, sticks, wires, roots, and other sharp objects that could puncture the pool liner.

Locate your pool where pool traffic will not cause problems in the main living area of your home or bother day sleepers. Keep your pool away from trees and other locations where leaves and other contaminants could cause problems to your pool's filter system.

Drive a long stake into the ground at the approximate center of the area to be used. Attach a string, which is 4 inches longer than the radius of your pool, and mark a circle on the grass. Remove all sod within the circular area. Leave the stake as a center mark.

LEVELING YOUR POOL

Using a straightedged 2 by 4, a carpenter's level, and a helper, locate the lowest point 6 inches inside the circle marked perimeter. Place one end of the 2 by 4 on the center stake and move the free end up and down over this lowest point until the level registers absolutely level. While maintaining the 2 by 4 at this level position, place a short board on this lowest point and attach it to the end of the 2 by 4. Refer to Figs. 4-2 through 4-4 as you level the pool area.

With the use of this depth leveling tool, remove a 1-foot wide strip of soil to this leveled depth around the inside of the circle. As you have surmised, the 2 by 4 rests on the stake and you remove soil until you have a level indication when the short board contacts the 1-foot wide strip. When you have leveled the 12-inch wide circle, remove the boarded nail to the 2 by 4.

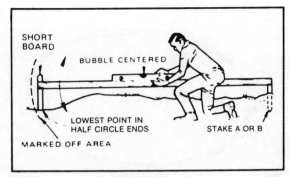

Fig. 4-3. Use a level and board to set up your pool area. Courtesy Doughboy Recreational, Inc.

By referencing from this level strip with the 2 by 4 and the level, remove all high areas until the entire pool area is smooth and level. *Don't* fill low spots in this area, as settling may cause your pool to become out of level.

If you wish, you may excavate the center area to the maximum depth as shown in Fig. 4-4. Be sure that the entire area is smooth and that all sharp stones and sticks have been removed

BEGINNING INSTALLATION

Using a string and the center stake, mark a circle in the earth the exact diameter of your pool, as shown in Fig. 4-5. Lay out the bottom rails inside the marked area with grooves *up*. Place a vertical end cap between each bottom rail. Slide the bottom rails into the vertical end cap until the rail is 1/16 inch from the stop in the vertical end cap. Continue around the pool until all bottom rails are joined together to form a complete ring.

Remember, if the soil is not completely firm, it is desirable that a patio block be placed flush with

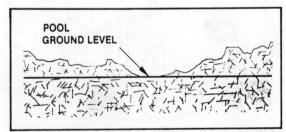

Fig. 4-2. Pool ground level should be the lowest point. Courtesy Doughboy Recreational, Inc.

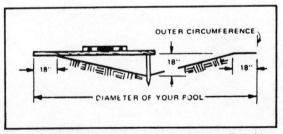

Fig. 4-4. Excavate to maximum depth. Courtesy Doughboy Recreational, Inc.

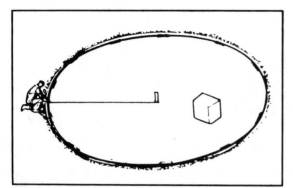

Fig. 4-5. Make a circle the exact diameter of your pool. Courtesy Doughboy Recreational, Inc.

Fig. 4-7. Bottom rail installation. Courtesy Doughboy Recreational, Inc.

the ground beneath each vertical end cap. Place the box containing the pool liner inside the ring of rails at this time to avoid having to lift it over the side wall later. If you have three or more people to help install the liner, leave it outside the pool.

INSTALLING THE SIDEWALL

Open the top of the sidewall carton, then turn the carton upside down and lift the box off the coil of steel contained inside. Before untying the cord

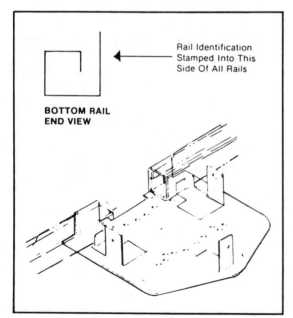

Fig. 4-6. Inserting the bottom edge in the rail. Courtesy Doughboy Recreational, Inc.

which holds the coil, look for an arrow along the end of the coil showing which end should be up. Begin unrolling the sidewall inside the bottom rings of the rails, starting at a point near to where you wish to locate your filter. On all pattern-coated walls, the white side should be inside. If you have a solid color wall, the white color wall is intended to be outside. If you prefer to turn the wall inside out, the pool will function with the joint piece on the inside of the pool, provided special care is taken so the liner will not be damaged. This includes taping all rough edges.

As you uncoil the wall, insert the bottom edge into the groove in the ring of bottom rails. Refer to Figs. 4-6 and 4-7. Start with the hook on the end of the wall centered in the vertical end cap nearest the filter location. As you insert the wall bottom into the groove in the rail, have a helper uncoil the

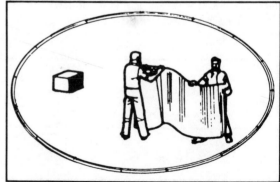

Fig. 4-8. Rest the wall on your foot as you guide it into the rail. Courtesy Doughboy Recreational, Inc.

sidewall about 6 feet ahead of you. Rest the wall on your foot as you guide it into the rail groove to maintain control (Fig. 4-8). If after the wall is completely into the rails you have a gap between the two ends of the wall, go around the pool and adjust the rails in the vertical end caps equally around the perimeter of the pool.

On a windy day, more than one helper will be needed to install the sidewall. On a pool with deep excavation, use these same steps, except uncoil the sidewall from outside the ring of bottom rails.

INSTALLING THE JOINT PIECE

Next, slip a short section of the sidewall, an equal amount on each side of the joint area, out of the groove in the bottom rails. Bring the ends of the sidewall tightly together as shown in Fig. 4-9. Then, slide the joint piece down over the formed hooks on the wall until the joint piece is even with the bottom of the wall. If the joint piece doesn't slide on easily, you don't have the sidewall ends lined up properly.

Insert the jointed sidewall back into the bottom rail. Measure the pool to be sure it is the correct size and shape. Tape all sharp edges in this area down inside of the wall about 2 inches and the outside about 1 inch. Use three or more thicknesses of tape (Fig. 4-10). Do not drive the joint piece on.

If included with your pool kit, install the large cover plate over the rectangular opening and small hole in the sidewall as illustrated in Fig. 4-11. This cover plate is intended to cover up the hole left for through-the-wall filtering and skimming equipment.

The stabilizer rails (Fig. 4-12) are installed next. Place a large diameter rail over the tape at the joint

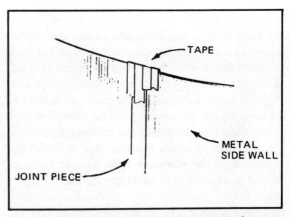

Fig. 4-10. Tape the sharp edges of the pool wall. Courtesy Doughboy Recreational, Inc.

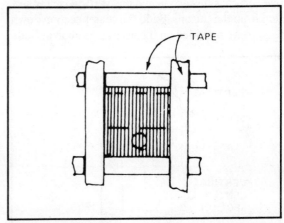

Fig. 4-11. Covering the wall hole with tape. Courtesy Doughboy Recreational, Inc.

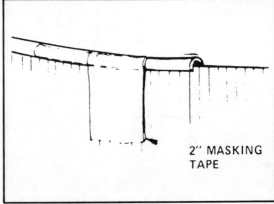

Fig. 4-12. Installing stabilizer rails. Courtesy Doughboy Recreational, Inc.

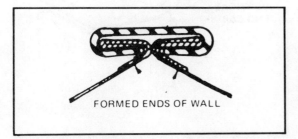

Fig. 4-9. Bring the ends tightly together. Courtesy Doughboy Recreational, Inc.

in the steel sidewall so that the rail is centered over the joint. Place a small rail next to one end of the large rail and insert it approximately 6 inches into the large rail. Continue in this manner, alternating the larger and smaller rails until all except the last rail is in place. To complete the circle, slide the remaining rail into the adjoining rail far enough so that it will slide into the rail in the opposite direction. Place a piece of 2-inch masking tape over the intersection of the stabilizer rails, as indicated, to secure placement until seats are installed.

INSTALLING VERTICALS

Refer to Fig. 4-13 illustrating a vertical. Take one vertical side section and one vertical center section from the cartons. Slide the center section down the groove provided on the section as shown. Slide another side section into the groove of the center section.

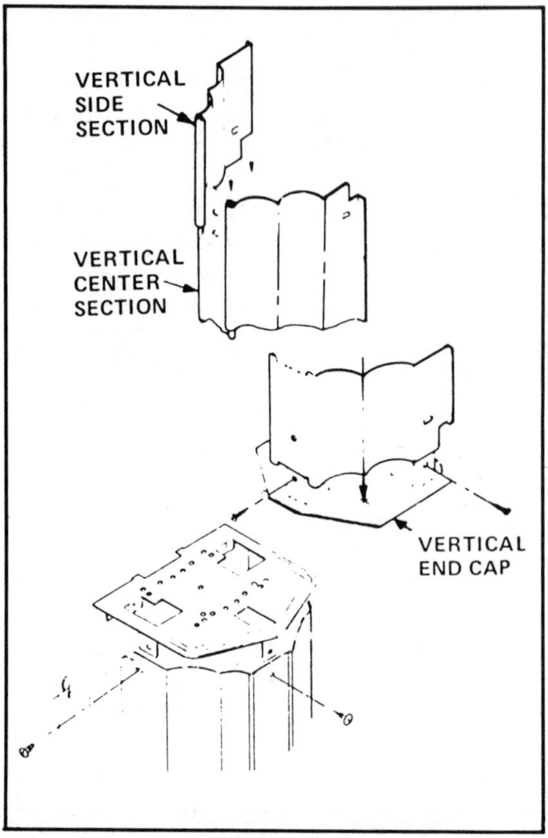

Next, place the assembled verticals on the vertical end caps so that all tabs on the caps are hidden inside the verticals. Attach the verticals to the caps using sheet metal screws. Attach the screw first through the vertical center section into the tab and then through the small slots on each vertical side section into the tabs.

Finally, place a vertical end cap over the top of each vertical, as shown, and hook the tabs over the stabilizer rail as this is done. Attach the cap with sheet metal screws through the vertical side sections and vertical center sections.

The rim or seat is installed next as illustrated in Fig. 4-14. Which hole you use to attach the seat to the cap depends upon the diameter of your pool. The figure illustrates installation for a 21-foot round pool. Holes for a 16-foot and 28-foot round pool are also shown. Figure 4-15 illustrates pool seats after installation. Figure 4-16 shows the hole pattern and support plate for a smaller 16-foot round pool offered by a leading manufacturer. After the rim or seat is installed, install the top connectors (Fig. 4-17).

![Fig. 4-13 illustration of assembling verticals showing vertical side section, vertical center section, and vertical end cap]

Fig. 4-13. Assembling verticals for your pool supports. Courtesy Doughboy Recreational, Inc.

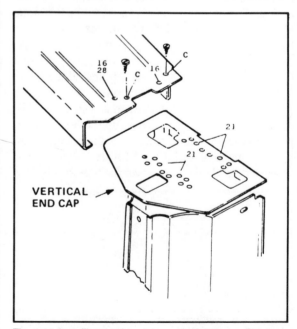

Fig. 4-14. Installing pool seat on vertical end cap. Courtesy Doughboy Recreational, Inc.

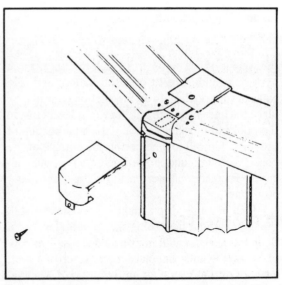

Fig. 4-15. Finished pool seat. Courtesy Doughboy Recreational, Inc.

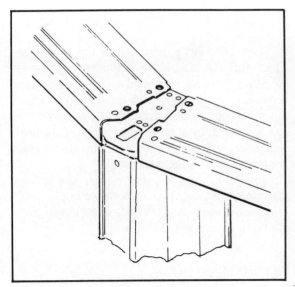

Fig. 4-17. Installing top connectors. Courtesy Doughboy Recreational, Inc.

INSTALLING THE LINER

Before you install the vinyl liner, recheck the pool for size and shape by measuring from the center to points around the bottom of the wall. Then carefully make a cove at the bottom inside edge of the wall using damp sifted earth (Fig. 4-18). Remove the center stake and fill the hole with earth. The cove is important in that it prevents the water pressure from forcing the pool liner under the bottom rail which might cause the liner to rupture. After leaving the pool, fill, tamp, and smooth out any depressions or footprints. It is important that

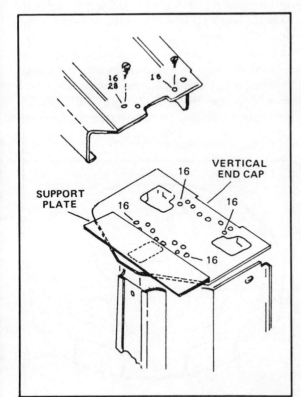

Fig. 4-16. Installing pool seats for 16-foot round pool. Courtesy Doughboy Recreational, Inc.

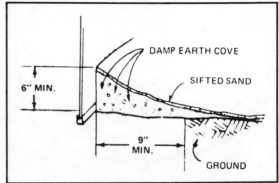

Fig. 4-18. Make sure the cove is sufficient to help support the pool wall. Courtesy Doughboy Recreational, Inc.

55

the liner be as smooth as possible when the pool is complete.

When installing the liner, the idea is to allow the weight of the water to stretch the liner into a perfect, wrinkle-free fit over the bottom and side walls of your pool. With an installation crew of two, place the liner near one edge of the sidewall inside the pool and unroll it carefully. Hand a portion of the liner sidewall to a helper on the outside of the pool. Proceed around the perimeter of the pool pulling the liner sidewall over the top of the frame about 30 inches.

Four or more people make it possible to install the liner without disturbing the smooth, level pool floor you have created in previous steps. Two people grasp the liner and place it on the top of a seat, away from the deep end, on round pools. On oval pools, opposite the deep end, place it on the middle of the end seat or the middle end vertical. The liner should have the loose end overhanging the outside of the seat about 1 foot and the rolled up section toward the pool. Hold on to the loose end of the liner and push the rolled section vigorously so that it will unroll (as you would unroll a carpet) down the middle of your pool.

Two people take the wall area of the liner and proceed in opposite directions around the pool. The other two follow and drape the liner wall over the seats and down the outside of the pool wall about 30 inches.

The embossed pattern side is the *water* side. The overhang should be adjusted so that it measures the same all around and so that the liner is touching the pool floor only in the middle. Before taping the liner to the uprights with 2-inch tape, correct any bunching or pleating condition of the liner wall. Also check that the bottom seams at side walls are centered with the pool wall.

Instead of tape, you may elect to use spring-activated wood clothes pins as shown in Fig. 4-19. Use one or two on the underside of each seat. Handle them as you would the tape.

FILLING YOUR POOL

It's time to add water. Carefully place a garden hose in the pool and begin to fill. As the pool fills, the liner should stretch when the water begins to cover the bottom (Fig. 4-20). At this time check the sidewall for extreme tautness. Any areas that feel tight should be relieved by releasing the tape and allowing the liner to feed back into the pool until the desired tautness is achieved. Retape before you proceed around the pool checking and retaping. Remember that you are monitoring a minimum tightness of liner over seat that will control the lin-

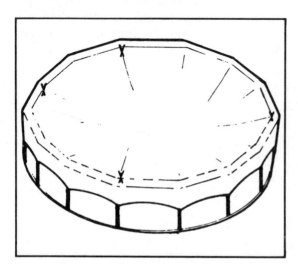

Fig. 4-19. Use spring-activated clothes pins to stretch the vinyl liner. Courtesy Doughboy Recreational, Inc.

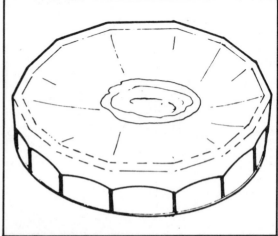

Fig. 4-20. Begin filling with water. Courtesy Doughboy Recreational, Inc.

Fig. 4-21. Stretch wrinkles and pleats out of the vinyl liner. Courtesy Doughboy Recreational, Inc.

er seating itself against the pool floor and up the side with no wrinkles.

Continue monitoring the liner tension as the water is approaching and covering the cove area of the pool. Be sure that the liner is evenly distributed over the seat without any bunching or pleating. If this is apparent, correct as you are adjusting the liner tension. When the water is approximately 6 inches deep or covering the cove, there should be just barely enough tension on the liner to control a wrinkle-free installation.

What should you do if there are wrinkles or pleats in the vinyl liner as you fill the pool? If this occurs, grasp the liner wall nearest this area and pull and lift just enough to stretch out these wrinkles or pleats (Fig. 4-21). It is easier if you wait until there is 1 to 2 inches of water over the wrinkled area before you try to remove them. This allows the weight of the water to hold the liner flat on the ground, keeping the wrinkles out after you remove them. Pull any excess liner over the seat and tape in position so that a minimum tautness will prevent any further wrinkling.

Double-check around the pool so that you have an even tension of the liner wall down to the liner floor. Don't attempt to lift and pull the liner if you have more than 4 inches of water in the wrinkled area. You could damage the liner.

Continue filling the pool. When the pool is about half full—2 feet—remove the top connectors, seats, and vertical end caps. Make sure the liner doesn't fall into the pool. If water should run between the wall and the liner you could damage the

pool or have to start over. It's best to use two or more people at this time. One person removes the liner from over the seats, the next person removes the seats, and the third person folds the excess liner inside between the metal sidewall and liner sidewall (Fig. 4-22). As this is done, remove the stabilizer rails from the top of the wall a section or two at a time. Pull up the wall of the liner firmly and smoothly so that it conforms to the metal sidewall, then fold 1 to 1 1/2 inches of this double layer of vinyl over the top of the wall. In this way, excess liner cannot be seen but is still available if needed in the future.

Place a 24-inch piece of plastic coping over this folded vinyl on the top of the metal sidewall as shown in Fig. 4-22. Continue around the perimeter of the pool in this manner. If bunching or gathering of the liner sidewall has occurred during this process, remove the coping two pieces at a time progressively around the pool smoothing wrinkles as you proceed. Adjust down as necessary to avoid excessive tension in the liner sidewall and replace plastic coping. Replace the stabilizer rails, vertical end caps, seats, and top connectors as previously instructed.

CHECKING YOUR POOL

Recheck the sidewall at this time to be sure that it is level by measuring down from the top of the

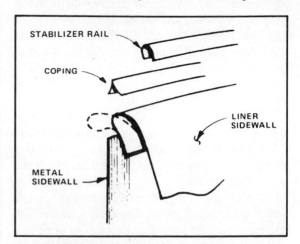

Fig. 4-22. Fold excess liner toward the inside of the pool. Courtesy Doughboy Recreational, Inc.

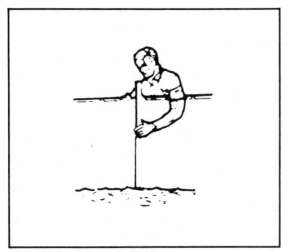

Fig. 4-23. Periodically check the depth of water around the pool. Courtesy Doughboy Recreational, Inc.

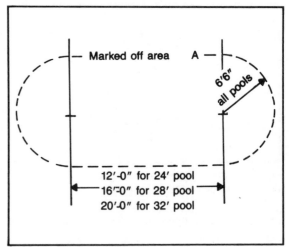

Fig. 4-24. Layout for an oval pool of various sizes. Courtesy Doughboy Recreational, Inc.

wall to the surface of the water at several points around the pool (Fig. 4-23). If the measurement varies more than 1 inch, the pool is not level. At the points where the measurement is longest, scrape away dirt under the bottom rail until the measurement is within the 1-inch tolerance. Be sure the bottom rails are lying flat on the ground with no humps or hollows beneath them.

Now you can fill your pool to the desired level. When the pool is filled, remove the hose as water may siphon from the pool into your water system. Don't make any permanent connections between your water system and the pool.

If a through-the-wall skimmer is to be installed, do this before filling with the last 2 feet of water. Once installed, frequently check the skimmer and return fitting screws for tightness to be sure there is no water leakage. Tighten as required.

Finally, place pool marker decals for the protection and safety of you and your guests. Peel backing paper off the decals to expose the adhesive surface. Attach each one to the pool liner with the top of the decal about 1 inch below the bottom edge of the seat inside the pool (see Chapter 10). Smooth and press firmly. The warning decals against diving are especially important as jumping or diving in any above-ground pool is dangerous and can result in great bodily harm.

INSTALLING AN OVAL ABOVE-GROUND POOL

Figure 4-24 illustrates a typical oval above-ground swimming pool. As you can see, it requires slightly different installation instructions than the round pool just covered. Let's consider these differences.

The oval pool has two radius stakes rather than one (Fig. 4-24). The pool's straight walls run between these two stakes—A and B. The layout then is simply making a round pool layout with a specified distance between the two halves of the circle. Figures 4-25 through 4-28 will help you develop

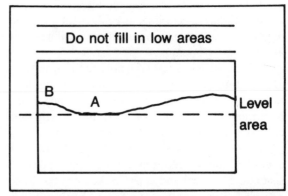

Fig. 4-25. Make sure the pool area is completely level. Courtesy Doughboy Recreational, Inc.

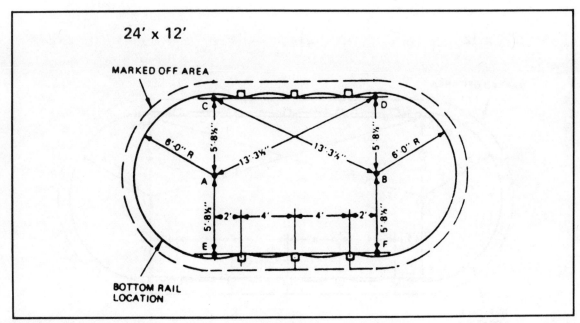

Fig. 4-26. Layout for a 24-×-12-foot oval pool. Courtesy Doughboy Recreational, Inc.

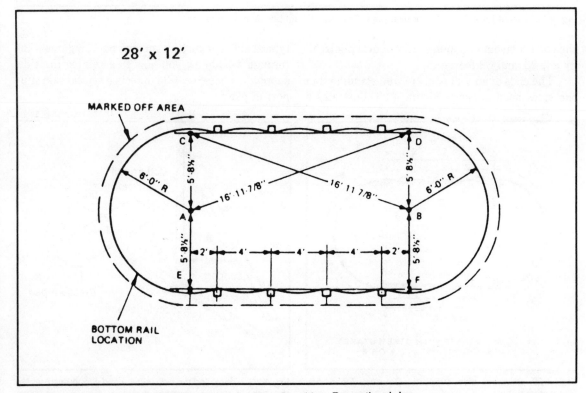

Fig. 4-27. Layout for a 28-×-12-foot oval pool. Courtesy Doughboy Recreational, Inc.

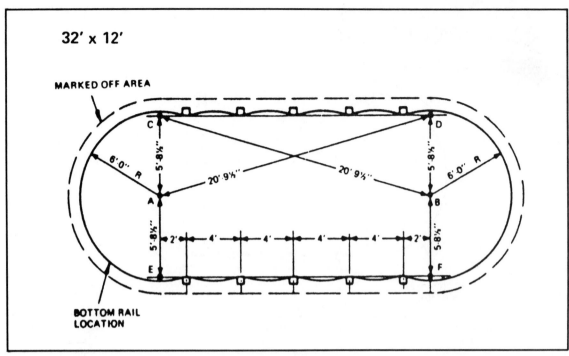

32' x 12'

MARKED OFF AREA

6'·0" R

5'·8½"

20'·9¼"

20'·9½"

5'·8½"

6'·0" R

5'·8½"

2' 4' 4' 4' 4' 2'

5'·8½"

BOTTOM RAIL LOCATION

Fig. 4-28. Layout for a 32-×-12-foot oval pool. Courtesy Doughboy Recreational, Inc.

the correct layout of popular sizes of oval pools: 12 by 24, 28, and 32 feet.

The ends of an oval pool are free-standing, but the sides need support. Figure 4-29 illustrates a typical side support for an oval pool. Figures 4-30 through 4-33 show you how to assemble the side supports. Then Fig. 4-34 depicts a typical side support in place.

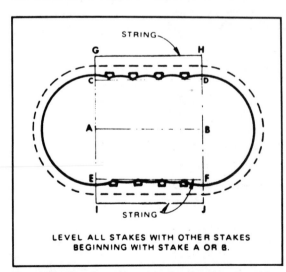

STRING

LEVEL ALL STAKES WITH OTHER STAKES
BEGINNING WITH STAKE A OR B.

Fig. 4-29. Planning side supports. Courtesy Doughboy Recreational, Inc.

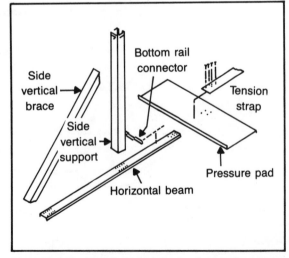

Bottom rail connector

Side vertical brace

Tension strap

Side vertical support

Pressure pad

Horizontal beam

Fig. 4-30. Assembling the side vertical and supporting braces. Courtesy Doughboy Recreational, Inc.

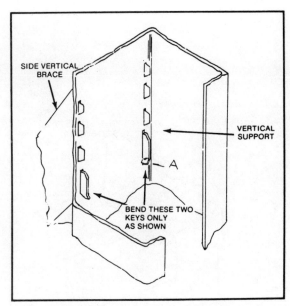

Fig. 4-31. Attaching side brace to vertical. Courtesy Doughboy Recreational, Inc.

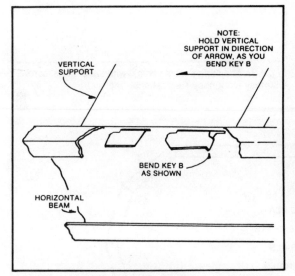

Fig. 4-32. Attaching vertical support to horizontal beam. Courtesy Doughboy Recreational, Inc.

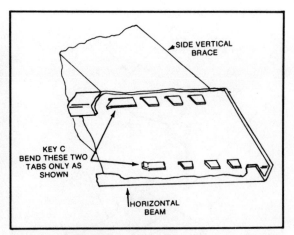

Fig. 4-33. Attaching side vertical to horizontal beam. Courtesy Doughboy Recreational, Inc.

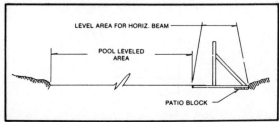

Fig. 4-34. Typical side support system. Courtesy Doughboy Recreational, Inc.

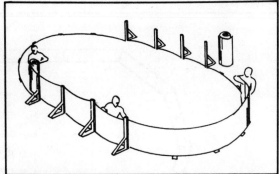

Fig. 4-35. Oval pool wall installation. Courtesy Doughboy Recreational, Inc.

The oval pool sidewall is normally installed much like that for the round pool. Larger oval pools have two-piece walls. They are installed in the same way except they have two joints rather than one (Fig. 4-35).

Seats on oval walls are also installed in a similar fashion. Refer to Figs. 4-36 through 4-39 for general instructions.

The vinyl liner is also installed much like that in a round pool. Figures 4-40 and 4-41 illustrate the

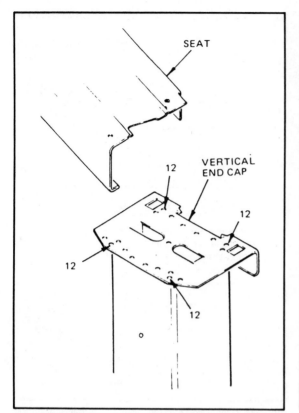

Fig. 4-36. Detail of seat installation. Courtesy Doughboy Recreational, Inc.

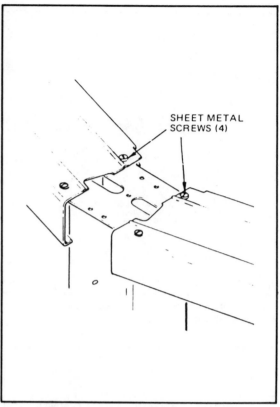

Fig. 4-37. Attaching seat to vertical with sheet metal screws. Courtesy Doughboy Recreational, Inc.

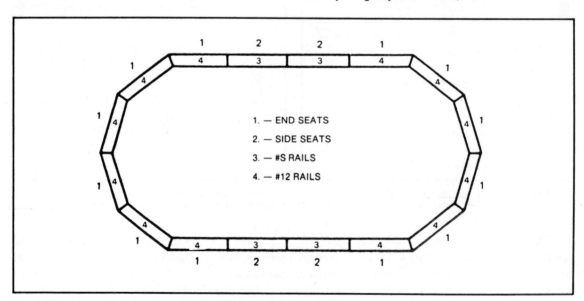

1. — END SEATS

2. — SIDE SEATS

3. — #S RAILS

4. — #12 RAILS

Fig. 4-38. Layout of oval pool. Courtesy Doughboy Recreational, Inc.

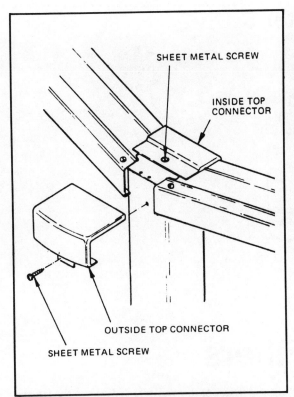

SHEET METAL SCREW

INSIDE TOP
CONNECTOR

OUTSIDE TOP CONNECTOR

SHEET METAL SCREW

Fig. 4-39. Installing inside and outside top connector on pool verticals. Courtesy Doughboy Recreational, Inc.

Fig. 4-40. Stretching the vinyl liner on a large oval pool. Courtesy Doughboy Recreational, Inc.

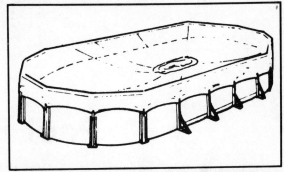

Fig. 4-41. Filling the pool with water. Courtesy Doughboy Recreational, Inc.

stretching and initial filling of an oval pool. The typical oval pool is larger than the round pool. You will probably need more help in installing the liner, making sure wrinkles are removed, and so that the liner doesn't fall in.

Finally, check for levelness. Complete the filling of the pool as you would the round pool.

Installing pool filter and heater systems for inground and above-ground pools will be covered in the next two chapters. Pool maintenance and repair, including how to repair vinyl liners, will be covered in Chapter 10.

Take a break and jump in the pool!

Chapter 5

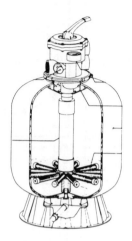

Pool Filters

A problem arises when you build a swimming pool. All this water sitting in one place soon begins to react to the world around it. The sun warms the water and makes it into an algae factory. Other organic and inorganic objects begin dotting the water's surface. What was designed as a swimming pool is now a stagnant pond.

How can you keep this from happening? By installing a system that will circulate the water and filter out impurities. This is the pool filter system.

Your pool's filter system is the only vital system within it. If necessary, you can—shudder—do without the pool heating system. Lighting isn't vital. But to keep your swimming pool swimmable you must have a water circulation and filtering system.

POOL FILTER SYSTEMS

A pool filtering system consists of four main elements (Fig. 5-1). These are the plumbing lines, which carry dirty water from the pool to the filter and water purified by the filter back to the pool; a pump for moving the water; the filter unit itself; and

a storm sewer or dry well which disposes the filtered matter. A fifth element used in many pools is the automatic skimmer, a device just below the water surface which insures that floating particles and substances are filtered.

POOL PLUMBING

Your pool's plumbing system depends on the requirements of your community, the size of your filter, and other factors. A major element is the main drain. This is an opening up to one foot in diameter located in the deep end of the pool in or near the floor, often under the diving board. This drain leads to the main suction line of the system which, in turn, leads to the filter.

There is also a return line to the pool. In a small pool this may lead to one inlet. In larger pools two inlets may be used. Inlets should be immediately below the water level and located so that the water naturally flows toward the main drain. When the inlets are properly located, there will be a gentle current in the pool.

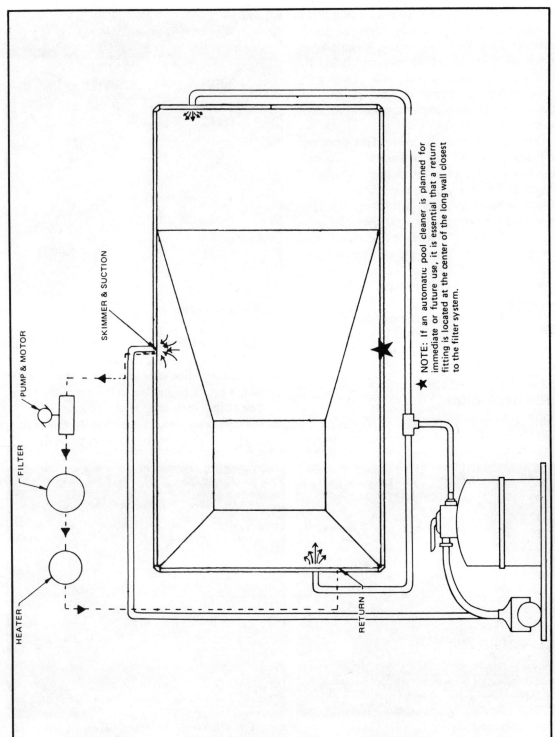

HEATER

FILTER

PUMP & MOTOR

SKIMMER & SUCTION

RETURN

★ NOTE: If an automatic pool cleaner is planned for immediate or future use, it is essential that a return fitting is located at the center of the long wall closest to the filter system.

Fig. 5-1. Typical pool filter and plumbing layout. Courtesy Heldor Associates, Inc.

Another opening in the pool may be a fitting to which the vacuum cleaning hose can be attached. This also leads to the filter. A fourth opening may be at the top of the wall, just below the water line. This opening is the one to which the automatic skimmer, if any, is attached. Both the vacuum line and the skimmer line are attached to the filter line.

Pool plumbing is usually made of plastic or copper. Plastic piping is low in cost and easy to install. It can be run in a shallow trench and isn't affected by freezing. Copper plumbing is best in areas where the soil is acidic. Pipe sizing varies depending upon the size and type of pool. Generally, smaller pools use piping of 1 to 1 1/2 inches in diameter. Larger pools use 1 1/2 to 2-inch pipes. The size also depends upon the distance between the filter and the pool. The greater the distance, the larger the pipe should be.

In installing pool filter system piping, minimize the number of turns and elbows. Install a valve on each line to make sure they can be isolated for maintenance and repair.

FILTER OPERATION

All these pipes lead to the pool's filter (Figs. 5-2 through 5-4). The filter itself consists of material

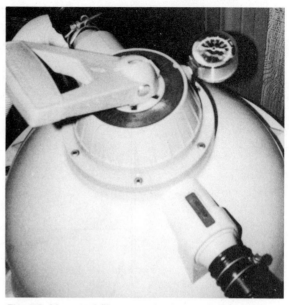

Fig. 5-3. Most pool filters are simple to operate.

through which the water passes. This screen can be made of one of several different substances. The most popular is fine sand and gravel. With such a system, water is brought in to the top of the filter. It then drips down over layers of sand 18 to 24 inches deep, over about 4 inches of the fine gravel, then layers of progressively coarser gravel. By the

Fig. 5-2. Typical pool filter.

Fig. 5-4. The filter should be located close to the pool so the return line is short.

time the water passes through this series, impurities have been filtered out. The *sand filter,* as it is called, operates much like the natural filtering system in a mountain stream feeding a lake.

Another popular filter material is *diatomaceous,* microscopic skeletons of tiny animals. Diatomaceous earth can filter everything down to about one-tenth of a micron. That's pretty fine.

SIZING YOUR FILTER SYSTEM

The size of your pool's filter system depends on many factors. The most important is the total number of gallons of water in the swimming pool (Fig. 5-5). To arrive at the capacity of your pool, multiply the cubic feet of water by 7.5—the number of gallons in a cubic foot.

The cycle is also important. The following sizing recommendations are based on a 12-hour to 16-hour cycle. This means that the pool water is completely cycled through the filter system within this period of time.

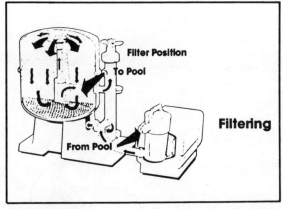

Fig. 5-6. Operation of typical sand filter. Courtesy Doughboy Recreational, Inc.

Smaller pools containing less than 18,000 gallons of water—such as 16 by 32 feet and smaller—can be adequately served by a sand filter (Figs. 5-6 through 5-10) 24 inches in diameter. For a medium sized pool of a 18,000 to 30,000-gallon capacity, a 30-inch diameter sand filter tank is cor-

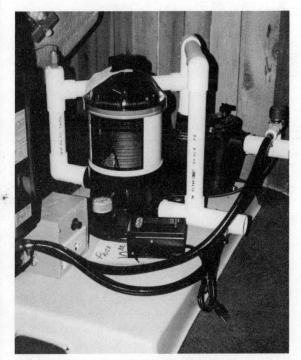

Fig. 5-5. Smaller pool filter system.

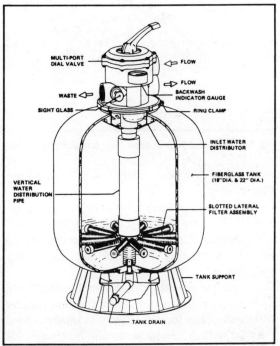

Fig. 5-7. Parts in a typical sand filter. Courtesy Richardson Industries, Inc.

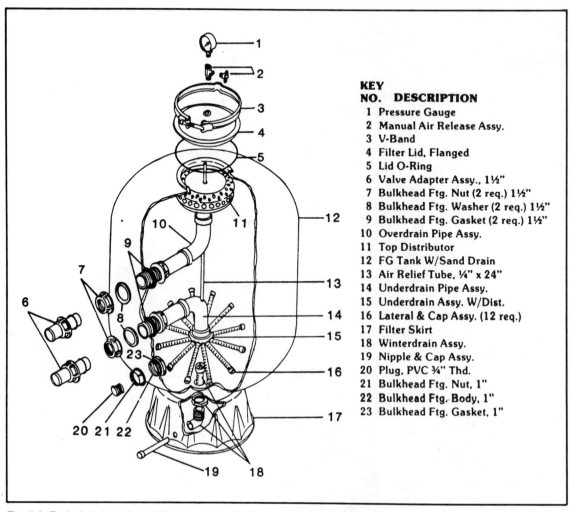

Fig. 5-8. Exploded view of sand filter components. Courtesy Richardson Industries, Inc.

rectly sized. Any pool larger than this should use a 36-inch diameter sand filter.

Diatomaceous earth filters are measured differently. They are measured in square feet of effective filter area. For most pools up to a 30,000-gallon capacity, a filter of 20 square feet is usually adequate.

There are several types of diatomaceous earth filters on the market today. One of the most popular is the skim filter located under a manhole behind the pool wall. A nearby pump and motor provide the suction to draw water from the main drain and skimmer opening through this filter. Other diatomaceous earth filters use fabric bags or replaceable cartridges to filter pool water.

The figures offered here on sizing your swimming pool's filter system are "typical." That means it'll always be higher or lower. Murphy's Law. Some days the filter system will be working hard filtering nothing. On weekends during the summer it will be striving to keep up with use. The best rule in sizing your filter system is to size it big using a "greatest use" estimate. Then purchase an adjustable filtering system that will allow you to increase the cycle time and reduce energy costs. This feature may save you many dollars.

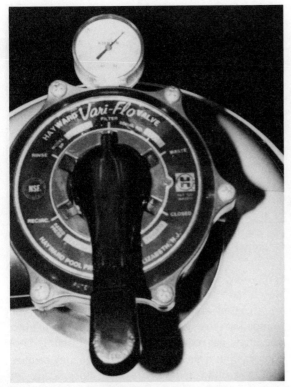

Fig. 5-9. The dial valve allows you to filter, rinse, recirculate, or direct waste easily.

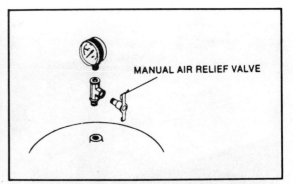

Fig. 5-10. Your filter should have a manual air relief valve so that excessive pressures do not build up in the filter. Courtesy Richardson Industries, Inc.

Paper filters are illustrated in Figs. 5-11 through 5-14.

BACKWASHING

Periodically, you must clean out your filtering system. This is done by *backwashing*. Both sand and diatomaceous earth filters require backwashing at regular intervals. In this process, water enters the filter from what is normally the outlet and pushes its way through what is normally the inlet section

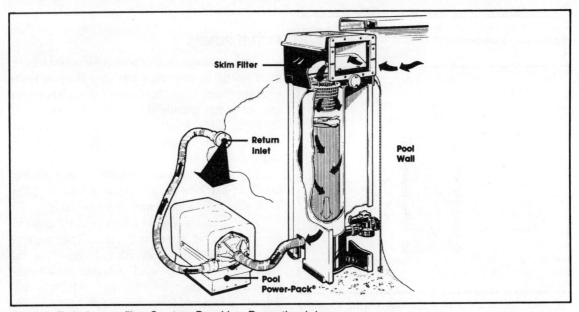

Fig. 5-11. Typical paper filter. Courtesy Doughboy Recreational, Inc.

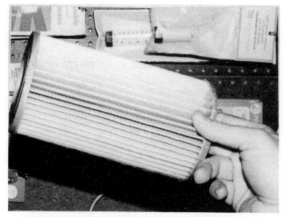

Fig. 5-12. Cartridge for paper filter.

Fig. 5-13. Cleaning the exterior of a cartridge filter. Courtesy Richardson Industries, Inc.

Fig. 5-14. Cleaning the cartridge filter interior. Courtesy Richardson Industries, Inc.

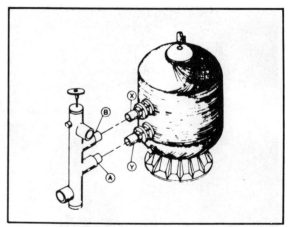

Fig. 5-15. Installing valve and piping for a backwash system. Courtesy Richardson Industries, Inc.

(Fig. 5-15). In doing this, it picks up the impurities which have been collected.

In rural areas, this backwash water may be dumped at the edge of your property. Closer to town you may be required to dump swimming pool backwash into the sewer. Other areas may require that you build a drywell system specifically for dumping the backwash. Be sure to check with local building and sanitary codes before installing such a system.

FILTER PUMPS

Both sand and diatomaceous filter systems require pumps to move the water from the pool to the filtering element and back to the pool. The pump and the motor usually set on concrete next to the filter (Fig. 5-16). A self-priming type is recommended so that air bubbles can pass through without causing an air lock.

Your pool filter pump will also have a strainer to collect particles before they pass into the filter. This strainer can be removed for cleaning.

How should you select a filter pump? Pumps for any job must be "sized" to the task. They must be selected according to the task to be done and the ability of the pump in mind. A higher *head*—water pressure per unit of area—and relatively low delivery is required for swimming pool filtering. Requirements for backflushing are different. The

Fig. 5-16. Pool filter pump.

pump must deliver three times the amount of water at a relatively lower pressure. In other words, the pump must operate well over a curve.

In most cases, your filter pump will be included with your filter system and sized by the designer. You may need to replace a filter pump in an existing pool, however. In this case, contact pump manufacturers or suppliers with details of your pool capacity, pipe, and filter sizes. They will be able to make recommendations based on these figures.

The pump is driven by a motor. The size of this motor depends on the size of the pool and other components in your filter system. For smaller pools, a 1/3-horsepower motor is normally adequate. For most residential pools, a 1/2-horsepower motor is sufficient to drive the filter pump. For larger pools, a 3/4-horsepower motor is usually installed.

As with filters, the motor that comes with your filter system is usually the best size. Otherwise, talk with pool suppliers about correctly sizing your motor.

POOL CLEANING EQUIPMENT

To keep your swimming pool from becoming a lily pond, pool cleaning equipment is necessary.

This includes pool skimmers and vacuum cleaners. These are actually part of the pool filtering system which supplies them with suction and collection.

The purpose of surface skimmers is to keep the surface of the water free from scum, oil, and other contaminants. There are two types of skimmers in common use. Wall skimmers and lily pad skimmers. Let's take a closer look at them.

Wall skimmers are mounted in the wall of your pool (Figs. 5-17 through 5-19). The water enters through one or more inlets and circulates around the pool. The mouth of the built-in wall skimmer is about 3 inches below the surface, and a plastic weir sticks up almost to the surface allowing a small amount of the circulating water to enter (Fig. 5-20).

The surface water first passes through a basket (Figs. 5-21 and 5-22) that removes any large particles. It is then sent to the pool filter through the skimmer line. An equalizer line is installed to avoid air locks which would stop the skimming action.

So-called "lily pad" skimmers attach to the

Fig. 5-17. The pool filter system should be located near the skimmer.

supported across the surface of the water with floats. Larger particles from the bottom are removed at the pump strainer. The water then passes through the filter where the smaller particles are entrapped.

Another type of pool cleaner, known as the jet type, uses a fine spray of water to pull particles up from the bottom of the pool. Debris is pulled up into a filter bag that can be cleaned at intervals.

WATER TREATMENT

A related aspect of pool filtering is the treatment of water to minimize the growth of algae and bacteria. Water filtration is a mechanical process. It removes suspended particles and keeps the water clear and inviting. Unfortunately, even clear and inviting water may contain disease-producing organisms in great number.

Fig. 5-18. Typical above-ground pool skimmer.

vacuum cleaner outlet just below the surface of the water. They operate similar to the wall skimmer except that the water returns to the filter through the vacuum line.

Another popular type of vacuum cleaner for pools consists of a head on wheels with a nylon brush which runs along the bottom of the pool. Water and contaminants from the pool floor are sucked in through a hose connected to the pool vacuum outlet. This type of pool cleaner is operated with a long handle from the pool deck, and the hose is

Fig. 5-19. Skimmer outlet is at the bottom.

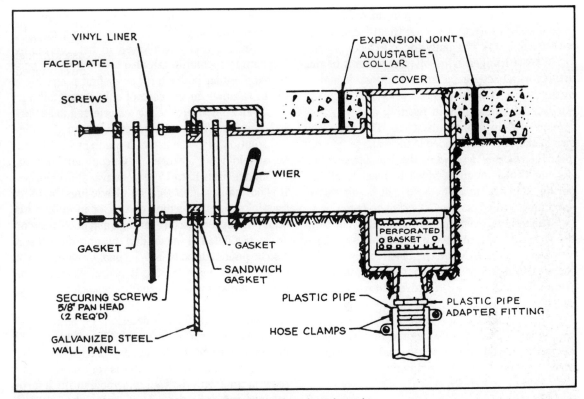

VINYL LINER
FACEPLATE
SCREWS
EXPANSION JOINT
ADJUSTABLE COLLAR
COVER
WIER
GASKET
GASKET
SANDWICH GASKET
PERFORATED BASKET
SECURING SCREWS
5/8" PAN HEAD
(2 REQ'D)
GALVANIZED STEEL
WALL PANEL
PLASTIC PIPE
HOSE CLAMPS
PLASTIC PIPE
ADAPTER FITTING

Fig. 5-20. Pool skimmer for in-ground pool. Courtesy Heldor Associates, Inc.

Chemical treatment of swimming pool water is the only satisfactory method of keeping it safe for human use. Chlorine, bromine, and iodine are most commonly used for controlling bacteria in swimming pools. These are all members of the chemical family called *halogens*. Chlorine and bromine can

Fig. 5-21. Skimmer baskets.

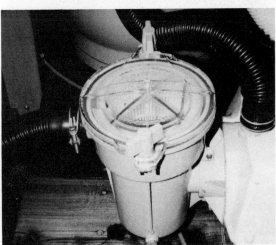

Fig. 5-22. Installed basket.

be introduced to water in the pure form or in the form of compounds that release them when mixed with water. Iodine is usually added as a compound.

When a halogen is dissolved in water it begins to react with bacteria and any other organic matter in the water. It oxidizes or "burns up" such impurities, but is used up in reacting and may also combine with inorganic substances. The amount of disinfecting chemical needed in the water is referred to as the *chlorine demand* or the *bromine demand.* If more than enough is added to react to all impurities initially present, there will be an excess remaining—called *residual chlorine* or *bromine.*

The residual chemical may be in its "free" form (free residual) or combined with another substance (combined residual). Some combined forms of these chemicals will kill bacteria, but the uncombined or "free" chemical is more effective and works much faster.

These residuals are measured in *parts per million,* or "ppm." You'll read and hear this term frequently as you purchase, test, and use chemical water treatments in your swimming pool.

CHLORINATION

Chlorine is the chemical most commonly used for killing bacteria in swimming pools. It can be added to the water in many ways. Relative advantages and disadvantages will also be covered.

Regardless of the compound used to produce chlorine in the pool, most authorities agree that a minimum residual of 0.6 parts per million free chlorine is necessary to assure safe pool water. A free chlorine residual of 1.0 to 1.5 ppm is often recommended.

Chlorine in its pure form at room temperature is a greenish, rather heavy, and very deadly gas. It is sold in high-pressure steel tanks because under such high pressure, it is actually a liquid in the tank.

Calcium hypochlorite is a dry white compound sold commercially in granular or tablet form. In water, it will yield about 35 percent hypochlorous acid or 70 percent (2 × weight) available chlorine. Calcium hypochlorite is easier to handle than chlorine gas, but it is nevertheless a strong oxidiz-

ing agent and care must be used to keep combustible materials away from it. The container must be kept covered and not allowed to become damp. Calcium hypochlorite can also be fed into the pool by hand, either in dry form or by first preparing a dilute solution, in the case of chlorinator failure.

Sodium hypochlorite is often referred to as "liquid chlorine." This chemical is sold as a clear liquid solution. It is the active ingredient in chlorine household liquid bleaches. In its commercial form, it contains from 10 to 15 percent available chlorine. It is normally sold in 1-gallon plastic jugs, 5-gallon plastic carboys, 55-gallon drums, or in bulk. This liquid can be fed directly through a hypochlorinator or can be diluted to any desired concentration. It can also be poured directly into the pool by hand in case of hypochlorinator failure. It has no sediment or precipitate and will not usually cause cloudiness in the water.

Sodium hypochlorite deteriorates, however, in sunlight and in warm conditions. Therefore it should be stored in a cool, dark place and used up as quickly as possible. If the pool water is very hard, it may react in time with the sodium hypochlorite to form calcium carbonate deposits at the point where the chlorinator tube enters the water line. It must be cleaned periodically with a hydrochloric acid solution.

Chlorinated isocyanurates offer stability of chlorine residual, ease of application, greater stability, and pH neutrality. They are available in granular and tablet form.

BROMINE

Bromine is a heavy liquid weighing about three times as much as water. It is volatile at room temperatures, and the heavy brown gas it forms is highly toxic. When a residual of 0.8 to 1.0 ppm is maintained in pool water, bacteriological studies show it to be as effective as chlorine in killing bacteria, at relative levels. Bromine is not widely used in swimming pool water treatment because of its higher cost and brownish color.

Iodine is an effective bactericide for swimming pool use, and its use causes less eye irritation than chlorination. Iodine at room temperature is crystalline in form and brownish in color, but pure iodine is seldom used for pool treatment. The usual method for treatment of pool water with iodine is to place an iodine compound, such as potassium iodide, into the water and then release the iodine as needed by the addition of chlorine. When chlorine comes in contact with potassium iodide, the chlorine drives iodine from the compound and takes its place in the compound. Iodine treatment is characterized by an iodine odor in the pool and a dark green color to the water. Iodine doesn't remove nitrogen from the water, so an algaecide is usually required. It is not widely used in swimming pool water treatment.

TESTING FOR RESIDUALS

The most common method for testing chlorine residual is the orthotolidine color test. It is based on the fact that orthotolidine reacts with chlorine to form a yellow-green color. This color is compared with known standards. The color produced by free chlorine appears within two seconds after mixing and must be compared immediately with the color sample provided. Chloramines and other chlorine compounds develop color with orthotolidine more slowly, and the final color developed measures the total chlorine.

Another method of testing for free chlorine directly is the Palin or DPD method. This is based on the use of diethyl-p-phenylene diamine. This method can also be used to measure individual chloramines in the pool water.

A third method for reading free chlorine as well as pH makes use of a simple test strip. In contact with the pool water, the test strip changes color, and the resulting color can be compared with standards. The test strip measures free chlorine only.

TESTING FOR pH

A measure of the degree of acidity of a solution on a scale of 1 to 14 (Fig. 5-23) is called pH. Distilled water has a pH of 7.0. Acids have a pH from 7.0 down to 1, the number decreasing as the acidity increases. Bases or alkalies have a pH from 7.0 to 14 in order of increasing strength. It can be seen that by adding alkali to water we raise the pH. Conversely, by adding acids the pH will be lowered below 7.

Most pool professionals recommend that pool water be kept at a pH range of 7.2 to 7.6—slightly alkaline. Many pool owners report safer feeling water, less eye irritation, and the ability to raise chlorine residuals without complaints by maintaining the pH at 7.5 to 8.0. It is believed that the great majority of eye irritation and complaints of too much chlorine are due not to chlorine, but to low pH, dissolved alum in the water, or chloramines.

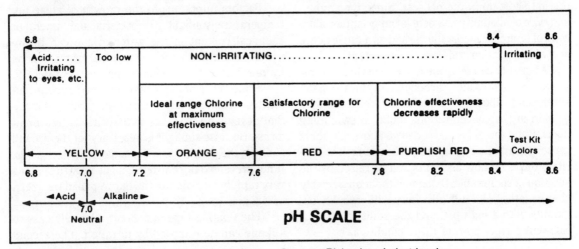

Fig. 5-23. The pH scale for swimming pool chlorination. Courtesy Richardson Industries, Inc.

Control of pH is relatively simple. The addition of soda ash—sodium carbonate—to the water raises the pH. The pH can be lowered by the addition of sodium bisulfate—sodium acid sulfate—in small amounts until the desired effect has been obtained. Hydrochloric (muriatic) acid is also used, but only with great care.

Determining the pH of pool water is a relatively simple operation. There are certain chemical dyes that are sensitive to acids and bases. The three most commonly used dyes or indicators are bromthymol blue (pH 6.0 to 7.6), phenol red (ph 6.8 to 8.4) and resol red (pH 7.2 to 8.8). Of the three, phenol red is most often used. The test is conducted with the same color comparator used for testing chlorine residual, except that a separate set of color standards and the proper indicator dye are used.

In water that has a very high chlorine content (1.0 ppm or over), the chlorine may bleach the pH indicator and give a false pH reading. In this case a drop of sodium thiosulfate (photographer's hypo) must be added to the vial before adding the indicator. The hypo reduces, or "neutralizes," the chlorine. Many indicator solutions already contain the neutralizer.

TESTING TOTAL ALKALINITY

Ionized alkalinity is indicated by pH. There is some un-ionized alkalinity in the water, and this doesn't show up in the pH test. Since the amount and type of alkalinity in a pool is important for alum control (granular media filters) and as a cause of eye and skin irritation, this test is important.

Alkalinity can take one or more of three forms. It can be hydroxide, carbonate, or bicarbonate. Bicarbonate alkalinity is not irritating to the eyes or skin in the concentrations found in swimming pools. But if the pH is allowed to go above 8.3, some carbonate alkalinity may be present which will irritate the eyes. Low alkalinity can be raised by the addition of sodium bicarbonate without appreciably changing the pH. High alkalinity will probably exist only with a high pH, and the addition of acid-sals will correct both of these conditions.

TESTING HARDNESS

Hardness and total alkalinity are related, but not identical. *Hardness of water* is the measure of calcium and magnesium compounds in the water. It may also be affected by some other metal ions, such as iron, aluminum, manganese, strontium, and zinc. *Carbonate hardness* is equivalent to total alkalinity. *Noncarbonate hardness* is of little interest to the pool owner.

Therefore, the total alkalinity test is usually sufficient for pool control, and hardness tests are seldom necessary. Problems with interfering metals, such as iron, should be solved by specific metal determinations rather than by the more general hardness test.

ALGAE

The complexity of the problem of controlling algae growth in swimming pool water is evident from the fact that 46 species of algae are designated as "clean water" algae. Some clean water algae are planktonic and float in the water. Others attach themselves to the floor and walls of the pool. Clean water algae types may be blue-green, green, red, brown, or even black.

Tastes, odors, cloudy water, slippery decks, and increased chlorine consumption may all be caused by algae. So it's important that the growth of algae in pools be conscientiously controlled.

Factors important to the growth of algae are temperature, sunlight, pH, bacteria, and mineral or chemical content in the water. Algae can be introduced to the pool in the original water source, by rain water, or by wind-borne dust and debris.

Some types of algae respond to treatment better than others, and there are even strains of algae that develop a resistance to the various treatment forms. Because sunlight is necessary for the growth of algae, the problem is more acute in outdoor pools. If not prevented or controlled, algae growth spreads very rapidly and can turn an entire pool dark green in a few hours.

The floating type of algae is relatively easy to kill and can be removed by filtration. The second type of algae, which attaches itself to the walls and grows in tiny crevaces, is often difficult to kill. If this type of algae gets a real foothold, there is only one solution: drain the pool and scrub it thoroughly with a stiff brush and a cleansing agent such as laundry detergent. As a last resort, muriatic acid or similar acid solution may have to be used. Once the algae growth has been removed, the pool can be refilled.

ALGAE CONTROL

There are several methods for treating algae, but by far the best and easiest method is to prevent its growth by maintaining a free chlorine residual at all times. When this fails to control algae, superchlorination is required. A pool that carries a free chlorine residual above 1.0 ppm continuously should have no algae trouble except where unusual conditions exist. A free chlorine residual is more effective than combined chlorine.

Frequent checking of pH can often head off algae trouble. A sudden unexplained rise in pH might very well tip you off that algae is in the water and growing fast before any visual sign is noticed. Prompt chlorine test followed by superchlorination often can head off the growth.

One of the oldest methods for killing algae is the use of copper sulfate. Though this chemical is cheap and effective, its use for algae control in pools is declining because when used to excess it is toxic to humans and may cause skin rash, dye the hair green, or cause staining of the pool surface. In water with considerable alkalinity, the copper sulfate causes a milky precipitate; and in water containing any sulphur, an inky precipitate will result. Other copper salts that are of lower toxicity and work better in alkaline waters are available under various trade names from pool suppliers.

Another group of algaecides, which seem to do a better job than copper sulfate without the same dangers, is the *quaternary ammonium halides* group of chemicals. Excess use of these compounds may cause foaming of the pool water and may interfere with the effectiveness of the chlorine disinfectant.

PROBLEM:	RESTRICTED WATER FLOW	FILTER PRESSURE BUILDUP	POOL WATER WON'T CLEAR UP
REMEDY	1. Check skimmer and pump strainer baskets for debris. 2. Check for restrictions in intake and discharge lines. 3. Check for air leak in intake line (indicated by bubbles returning to pool). 4. Backwash filter.	1. Check for algae in pool and superchlorinate as required. 2. Be sure chlorine and pH levels are in proper range and (adjust as required). 3. Check surface of filter sand bed for crusting. Remove 1" sand if necessary).	1. Check chlorine, pH and total alkalinity levels and adjust as required. 2. Be sure flow rate through filter is sufficient. 3. Operate filter for longer periods. 4. Be sure valve is set at "Filter" position.

POOL CHEMISTRY GUIDELINES		
SUGGESTED POOL CHEMISTRY LEVELS	ACTION REQUIRED TO CORRECT POOL CHEMISTRY	
	TO RAISE	TO LOWER
pH 7.2 to 7.6	Add pH up*	Add pH down*
TOTAL ALKALINITY Concrete 80 to 120 ppm Vinyl/Fiberglass 80 to 150 ppm	Add Alkalinity up*	Add pH down*
CALCIUM HARDNESS 100 to 200 ppm	Add Calcium Elevator*	Dilution--partially drain & refill pool
CHLORINE (STABILIZED) 1.0 to 2.0 ppm	Add chlorine	No action--chlorine will naturally dissipate
CLOR-SAVE STABILIZER (Cyanuric Acid) 40 to 100 ppm	Add CYA Stabilizer	Dilution--partially drain & refill pool with water that has not been treated with stabilizer

Fig. 5-24. Filter troubleshooting guide and pool chemistry guidelines. Courtesy Richardson Industries, Inc.

The quaternary ammonia halides are used extensively today as algaecide, but still don't provide the ultimate answer to the problem. They have a tendency to absorb on filter media and disappear rapidly from the water. They also may increase the chlorine demand when in the pool. Also, some strains of algae actually develop a resistance to these compounds.

All the chlorine disinfectants that provide free available chlorine are excellent algaecides. They are widely used to kill algae in swimming pools.

Further information on maintaining pool filters, pumps, cleaning equipment, chlorinators, and water conditions will be covered in Chapter 9. Figure 5-24 shows a troubleshooting guide. Next, we need to warm up the water for swimming.

Chapter 6

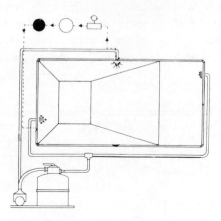

Pool Heating

Is a pool heater a necessity or a luxury?

Every pool owner asks this question at least twice: once before pool installation and once sometime thereafter. The answers each time should be the same—but often are not.

The purpose of this chapter is to help you answer this question for yourself. Then, if the answer is "a necessity," the chapter will show you what you can do about it.

PRO AND CON

Like most everything else, the question of installing a pool heater comes down to dollars and sense. Heaters are an added expense both during installation and operation. Just how many dollars depends upon the size of your pool, the local climate, your swimming season, local utility rates, the efficiency of your heating system, and numerous other factors.

Considering the other side, a pool heater can increase your home swimming season as much as 50 percent. You can enjoy your pool an additional

two months in the spring and fall in cooler climates or even year round in warmer climate areas. You can also extend your swimming day, making morning and evening swims more pleasant. Even if you decide against installing a heater, you may want to do some of the primary plumbing for it, just in case you or the next owner decide otherwise (Fig. 6-1).

POOL HEATER BASICS

Consider your swimming pool a huge water tank, which it is. To make it a hot water tank like the one in your home you must have a method of measuring and controlling the warmth of the water. This is your pool heating system. The major difference between a home hot water tank and a swimming pool's water heating system is the size: 30 gallons compared to, perhaps, 30,000 gallons.

One reason why pool heating can be so expensive is water's high heat capacity. It takes a relatively large amount of heat to raise a gallon of water one degree in temperature. With a swimming pool, there is also a fairly large heat loss to the colder air around it.

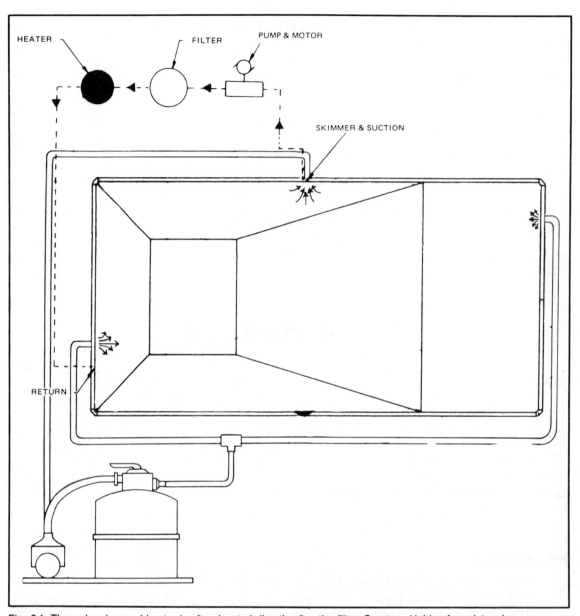

HEATER FILTER PUMP & MOTOR

SKIMMER & SUCTION

RETURN

Fig. 6-1. The swimming pool heater is often located directly after the filter. Courtesy Heldor Associates, Inc.

Because of the thousands of gallons that must be heated in even the smallest pool, you can't decide to turn on the heater an hour or so before you take a plunge. You will have to allow at least 24 hours for the water to reach the point where it will be comfortable. The actual time needed depends on the heater and the rise in temperature required.

There are many types of pool heaters in use today (Fig. 6-2). With direct-type heaters, the water is heated in pipes as it passes through, usually by gas burners. With the indirect type, the pipes carrying the pool water pass through a boiler containing hot water heated by the burners. Heat exchanger pool heaters are also popular.

Both the direct and indirect heaters operate off the main line of the pool. Some of the water from the filter is diverted into the heater where it absorbs the heat and then flows back into the pool through the return line. Since the heater utilizes the filter system with its pump, both the filter and the heater have to run at the same time.

Another kind of swimming pool heater operates on the radiant heat principle. A circuit of 1/2-inch copper tubing is embedded in the walls and floor of the pool. The circuit is connected to a boiler and circulates hot water through the sides and floor of the pool. The heat from the tubing radiates to the walls and bottom of the pool and is transferred to the water. The radiant heating system must be in-stalled when the pool is being built. It is suitable only for poured concrete, Gunite, or hand-packed concrete pools.

SELECTING THE HEATER

The type of swimming pool heater you select will depend greatly upon what utility is the least costly and most available in your area and at your pool site: gas, oil, or electricity (Figs. 6-3 through 6-5). Selecting between direct and indirect is more a matter of personal preference and product availability. It's smartest to select what most other pool owners in your area have. It's both proven and maintainable.

Next comes sizing. The considerations are time and temperature. Heating time is an important factor in determining heater size. Generally, a 24-hour period is recommended as being most satisfactory and economical.

A good rule of thumb is assuming that you will want to increase the temperature of your pool by 20 degrees over a 24-hour period. You must also allow for some heat loss to the ground and air. Taking this heat loss into account, choose a heater that will heat the amount of water you have in your pool at the rate of *one degree per hour.* Under most conditions, this should give you a 20-degree increase over a 24-hour period.

The other factor you must know is the dimensions of your pool. As an example, let's say your pool is 20 feet wide, 38 feet long, with an average depth of 6 feet. A final temperature of 75° F. is desired within 24 hours from pool-filling time. The average water temperature is 55° F., for example, so the desired temperature rise will be about 20 degrees.

The number of gallons of water in the pool is found by multiplying 20 by 38 by 6 by 7.5 (cubic feet per gallon). The answer is 34,200 gallons of water in your pool.

The total heat required is found by multiplying the gallonage by the pounds per gallon by the temperature increase desired. The answer is in *BTUs,* or *British Thermal Units,* the primary heat measurement. For our example, the problem reads:

Fig. 6-2. Gas-fired pool heater.

$$34,200 \times 8.33 \times 20 \text{ degrees} = 5,697,720 \text{ BTU.}$$

Fig. 6-3. The pool heater can be located in the pool filter house. Courtesy NSPI.

Fig. 6-4. The pool heater can also be located within the home if near the pool. Courtesy NSPI.

Now to figure the heat required per hour of operation, divide this figure by 20 hours.

$$5{,}697{,}720 \div 20 = 248{,}886 \text{ BTU heater output capacity.}$$

You might also select a heater with a listed output rating based on a 20-degree temperature rise of 1710 gallons per hour (pool gallonage divided by 20).

Actually, this method of sizing a heater for your pool will give you an oversize unit that heats the water comparatively quickly. In the interest of economy, you could choose a heater with one half or even one third of this recommended output capacity and still get a lot of off-season use from your pool. With a smaller unit you can maintain the temperature of the pool for a month or two into the fall, but will find it more difficult to heat it in the early spring. An enclosure, discussed in Chapter 8, or the regular use of a pool cover will do much to help hold the heat in the pool.

EFFICIENT HEATER OPERATION

You may find that your swimming pool will be used only on the weekends or heavily during a short period of the year (Fig. 6-6). In these and similar cases it may be more efficient to maintain your pool's heating system at a lower temperature when not in use.

As an example, let's say your pool will normally be used between Friday evening and Sunday afternoon. During this time you've decided to maintain pool water temperature at approximately 80° F. By lowering the water temperature to 70° F. during the rest of the week you are saving energy while

Fig. 6-5. An adjacent bath house is often used to house the pool's heating and filtration equipment. Courtesy NSPI.

Fig. 6-6. If your pool is only used on the weekends, you may decide to turn off your heater until Friday afternoon. Courtesy NSPI.

Fig. 6-7. A pool that is often shaded from the sun's rays will require a bigger heater than one located in the open sun. Courtesy NSPI.

still having warm water no more than 10 hours away. That is, you can turn the pool heater up to 80° F. early Friday morning, and it should be warm enough by late Friday afternoon.

If you swim more frequently than this you may wish to maintain the water temperature at or slightly below your ideal swimming temperature. If you use the pool less frequently or plan to have extended unused time, you should maintain the water temperature at or under 70° F.

What's the "best" pool water temperature for swimming? Like selecting the "best" pool, the answer depends on many things: local humidity level, wind chill, amount of direct sun or shade (Figs. 6-7 and 6-8), and personal preference. Many pools are maintained at 75° F. for relatively comfortable swimming, while others need 85° F. The best starting point is approximately 80° F. with adjustments made for individual needs and weather conditions.

HELPING YOUR HEATER

There are a number of things you can do to help your swimming pool heater do its job more efficiently and economically. The first is to keep a floating thermometer in your pool. It will give you an accurate reading of water temperature and help you decide the best pool temperature for your swimming comfort.

Keep your thermostat at the lowest comfortable setting. Each degree Fahrenheit of heat could add 10 percent or more to your fuel bill. Also, mark the comfort setting on the thermostat dial to insure that the temperature is not forgotten. This will also help prevent accidental or careless overheating.

Plan ahead. Lower the pool thermostat to 70° F. when the pool will not be used for three or more days. This will save you energy costs on unused heat.

Wind can evaporate water quickly and draw heat from your pool. Protect your pool from any winds beyond a breeze. A fence or outbuilding can serve this purpose. (Refer to my book *The Complete Book of Fences* (TAB Book No. 1508).

Remember to winterize your heater by draining it prior to freezing weather. This is also a good time to have a maintenance checkup done or to do it yourself. Check all fittings, valve operation, pip-

Fig. 6-8. This pool gathers direct sun most of the year. Courtesy NSPI.

ing, thermostat, and other elements to insure that, come spring, your pool will be ready to heat and enjoy. Information on winterizing your swimming pool will be offered in Chapter 10.

POOL COVERS

Once you have heated your swimming pool, it makes sense to put a lid on heat loss when you're not using the pool. This "lid" is often a pool cover (Fig. 6-9).

Typical swimming pool covers come in a variety of types. The simplest is a sheet of lightweight black polyethylene plastic cut to size and spread over the water. Better covers include polypropylene mesh suspended above the water (Figs. 6-10 through 6-12) and vinyl-laminated dacron that lays on top of the water. These are normally anchored to the edge of the pool using a rope or spring system. There are also numerous brands and types of retractable swimming pool covers. Some are manual and some automatic with a drive motor to draw the cover over the water.

The type of pool cover you choose depends on many factors. The first is your budget. Is the added cost of such a cover worthwhile based on energy

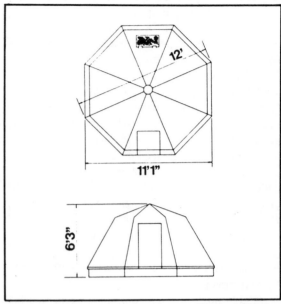

Fig. 6-10. Small suspended pool cover. Courtesy Fabrico Manufacturing Corp.

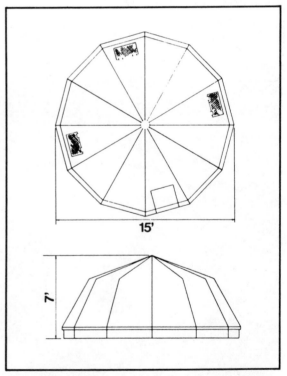

Fig. 6-11. Suspended pool cover for 15-foot round pool. Courtesy Fabrico Manufacturing Corp.

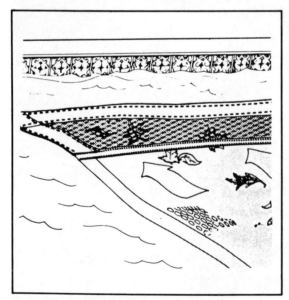

Fig. 6-9. Typical floating pool cover. Courtesy Richardson Industries, Inc.

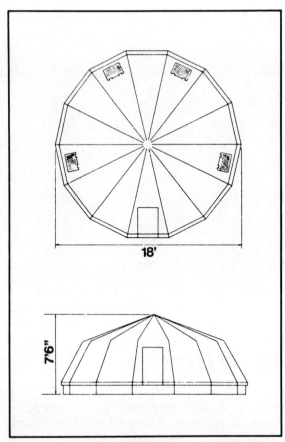

Fig. 6-12. Larger suspended pool cover for 18-foot round pool. Courtesy Fabrico Manufacturing Corp.

savings? You must consider the amount of heat loss, your usage of the pool, and other factors. An inexpensive, yet efficient pool cover may pay for itself in one or two seasons.

Safety is another factor. A sheet of plastic spread over a swimming pool may become a hazard as a visitor or child attempts to walk across it unaware. This is the best case in favor of an anchored pool cover.

Of course, much depends on your family's swimming habits. A pool cover that is difficult to remove and store may become a deterrent to a "quick swim." So the pool cover you select should be one that is easy to place and remove. One popular method is to install the pool cover on a pipe that is wider than the pool and can be rolled or unrolled over the surface as needed.

ALTERNATIVE HEATING

There is another popular method of heating swimming pool water that has become increasingly popular in the last decade: solar heating. It has many advantages over conventional pool heating systems and, after the initial cost, can be a low-cost system offering warm swimming water almost year round in some areas of the country. Chapter 7 will cover solar pool heaters and other aspects of the solar pool.

Chapter 7

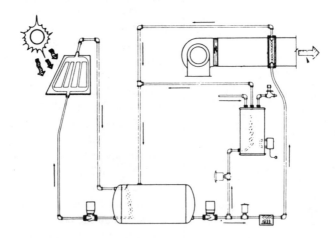

The Solar Pool

Unheated swimming pools are only comfortable for a few months of the year in most of the United States. Only rarely is the water warm enough for extended swimming in the evening or early morning.

The temperature requirements for swimming depend on a number of things. For short periods, or after a sauna bath, almost any temperature is acceptable. Pools used for competitive swimming are usually kept around 72° F. Most recreational swimmers feel more comfortable at around 80° F. For early morning or evening swimming when the air is cool, 85° F. or higher is desirable. Small children require temperatures of 85° F. or more to be able to swim any length of time without shivering. They tend to cool off rapidly because of their large surface-area-to-weight ratio.

As you've learned, a permanent swimming pool can be a major financial investment, require year-round maintenance, and take up a significant amount of yard space. Yet the pool is only useful for a few months of the year without heating. It

makes sense, then, to invest in pool heating to increase the usefulness of the pool's initial investment, maintenance, and land area.

You've also learned that pool heating, like pool ownership, costs money. A pool has high natural heat losses caused by thermal radiation, convection, and evaporation. If you want the pool temperature to be higher than nature wants it to be, you have to pour in heat on a virtually continuous basis to make up for the natural heat losses. This takes heavy-duty—and expensive—heating equipment plus large amounts of heat energy. Heating bills for swimming pools usually run over $30 a month and can often run two or three times that amount.

What's the solution? Heating a swimming pool is an ideal use for solar energy (Figs. 7-1 and 7-2). The heat is needed at low temperatures, so simple collector designs can be used. A pool is equipped with a filter and circulation pump, so a solar heat collector can be supplied with a large flow rate of filtered water. Pool water is normally treated, so it is of dependable chemistry. Temporary bad weath-

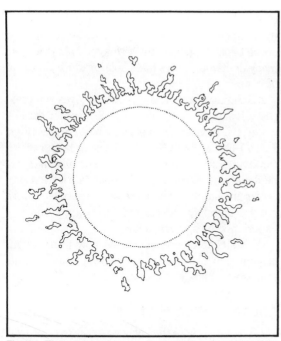

Fig. 7-1. The sun can be your best source of pool heating. Courtesy U.S. Department of Energy.

er is not too bothersome; the effectiveness of solar heating is reduced, but swimming desires normally fluctuate in phase with the weather. Most other applications of solar energy are not only more difficult, but also more demanding.

So let's take a closer look at heating your pool with solar energy.

THE SOLAR SOURCE

Solar energy is not new. Agriculture, mining of fossil fuels, the use of windmills all involve the collection of what was once solar energy. Nuclear energy and geothermal energy are probably the only energy sources commonly used which can not be traced back to the sun.

Solar energy has been used to heat water for many years, and the design requirements of solar water heating equipment have been studied for more than 40 years. The lack of widespread application has not been due to lack of understanding. It is simply that up to this time other sources of energy have been so economical. This has limited interest

Fig. 7-2. A body of water can gather the direct rays of the sun for natural solar heating. Courtesy Western Wood Products Assn.

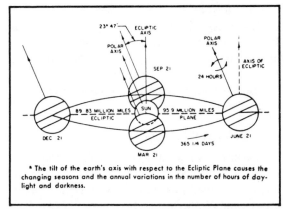

* The tilt of the earth's axis with respect to the Ecliptic Plane causes the changing seasons and the annual variations in the number of hours of daylight and darkness.

Fig. 7-3. Actual motion of the earth about the sun. Courtesy National Science Foundation.

in solar water heating to those with the understanding and enthusiasm necessary to build their own equipment.

Copper is the ideal material for solar water heaters. It does not corrode, except in some very few cases in which the water has aggressive impurities. It has a very high thermal conductivity. It is easy to cut, bend, and solder. It lends itself to sim-

ple heater designs and easy assembly. It is virtually unaffected by the atmosphere or by sunlight. It doesn't rust or get brittle with age. This is why so many do-it-yourselfers build solar water heaters out of copper.

Building a solar heater yourself gives you great cost advantages. The only expenses are for the raw materials. In most parts of the United States (Figs. 7-3 to 7-6) it is possible to build a solar heater which can heat a swimming pool more cheaply than can be done with natural gas. Copper fabrication processes are simple enough so that it is possible to turn out a professional looking job with a minimum of experience or special tooling.

This chapter will show you how to heat your swimming pool as cheaply as possible using a home-built solar energy collector.

SOLAR HEATER PHYSICS

The function of the solar heater is to collect the solar energy incident on a large area and to transfer this to the pool water at a minimum cost. One could simply cover the area with blackened tubes so that

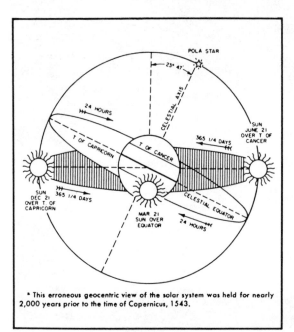

* This erroneous geocentric view of the solar system was held for nearly 2,000 years prior to the time of Copernicus, 1543.

Fig. 7-4. Apparent annual motion of the sun about the earth Courtesy National Science Foundation.

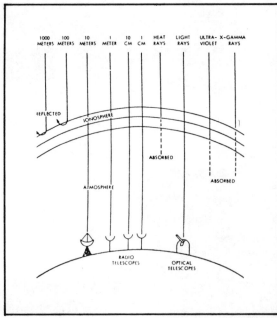

Fig. 7-5. Solar rays in the earth's atmosphere. Courtesy U.S. Department of Energy.

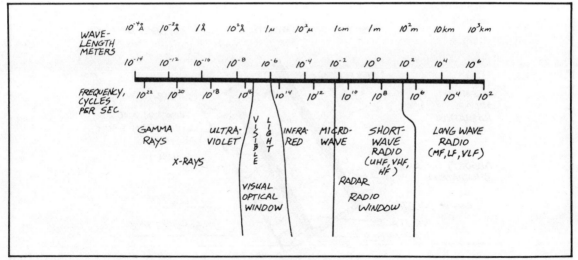

Fig. 7-6. The wavelength spectrum. Courtesy U.S. Department of Energy.

all the sunlight would fall on the tubes. But this would be too expensive. You could also use lenses or mirrors to concentrate the energy on tubes spaced some distance apart. This method is also too expensive, except when collecting the energy at high temperatures, as the concentrators must follow the sun.

The most economic way to collect the solar energy for swimming pools seems to be with the so-called flat plate collector. This was developed more than 40 years ago and has been built, tested, refined, and analyzed by many people over the years. It generally consists of tubes fastened at regular intervals to a flat sheet of highly conductive metal as shown in Fig. 7-7. The whole assembly is given a coating which will absorb sunlight. It can also be covered with one or more layers of glass or transparent plastic, and it can be insulated in the back to prevent heat losses. Both are necessary when you want to get high-temperature water.

The operation of such a panel is quite simple in concept (Figs. 7-8 to 7-11). Solar energy heats up the sheet (or fins) and the tubes. Some of this solar energy is lost back to the atmosphere, but hopeful-

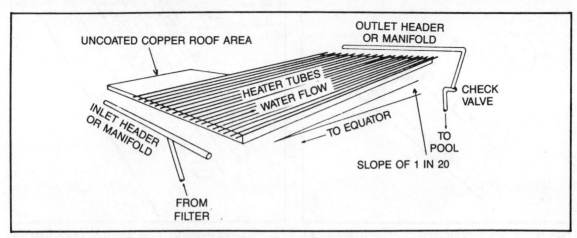

Fig. 7-7. Typical solar collection panel. Courtesy Brace Research Institute.

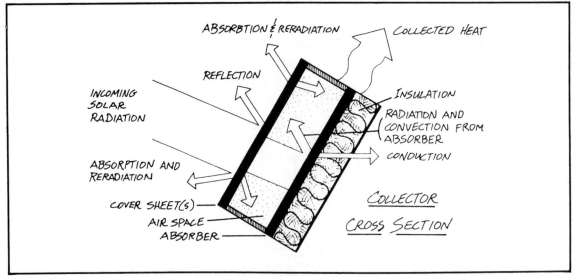

Fig. 7-8. How the solar collector works. Courtesy U.S. Department of Energy.

ly most of it ends up in the water. The part falling on the tubes is conducted directly through the tube wall and transferred to the water. The part falling on the fins heats the fins locally so that they become warmer than the tubes, with the result that heat flows towards the tubes. If the fins are too long and thin, they will heat up excessively and too much solar energy will be lost back to the air rather than going into the water.

The performance of the panel is also affected by panel inclination, latitude, weather, time of year, and by the effectiveness of the radiation coating (Figs. 7-12 through 7-17). All of these can be calculated. The weather is, however, pretty random and, at best, only statistically predictable.

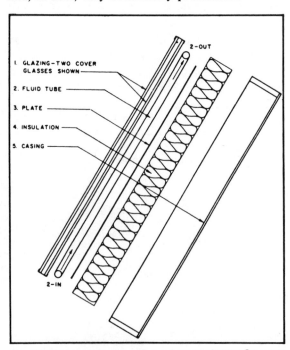

Fig. 7-9. Solar rays strike the collector, warming the medium. Courtesy U.S. Department of Energy.

Fig. 7-10. Cross section through a solar water heater. Courtesy National Science Foundation.

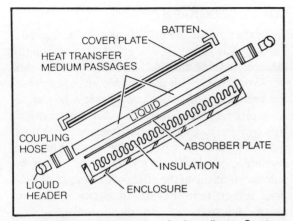

Fig. 7-11. Detailed cross section of solar collector. Courtesy U.S. Department of Energy.

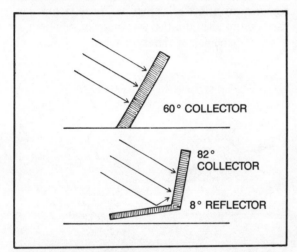

Fig. 7-12. Collector performance is affected by inclination. U.S. Department of Energy.

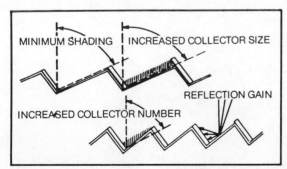

Fig. 7-13. Collector inclination guidelines. Courtesy U.S. Department of Energy.

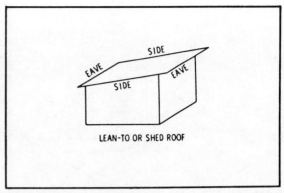

Fig. 7-14. Collectors can be located on a shed roof. Courtesy Brace Research Institute.

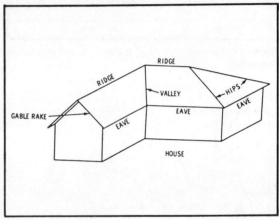

Fig. 7-15. Terminology used in roof construction. Courtesy Brace Research Institute.

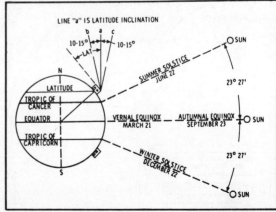

Fig. 7-16. Position of the sun in the sky at noon and its relation to the inclination and location of the collector. Courtesy Brace Research Institute.

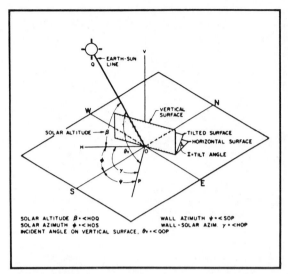

Fig. 7-17. Solar position angles. Courtesy National Science Foundation.

SOLAR GEOGRAPHY

If the atmosphere didn't exist, or if it didn't influence solar radiation, the effect of geographical location would be simple. The solar input each day would only vary with the latitude and the time of the year. The only complication might be that in some places mountains or other obstructions might help by reflecting extra sunlight our way, or might reduce inputs by casting shadows. Otherwise everything would be simple. It would in fact be possible to calculate the effect of geographical location, rather than having to depend fully on measurements.

Unfortunately things are not that simple. Cloud cover, atmospheric dust, smog, or smoke can significantly affect solar inputs. These factors can vary due to altitude; the proximity of mountains, deserts, or bodies of water; or urban or industrial

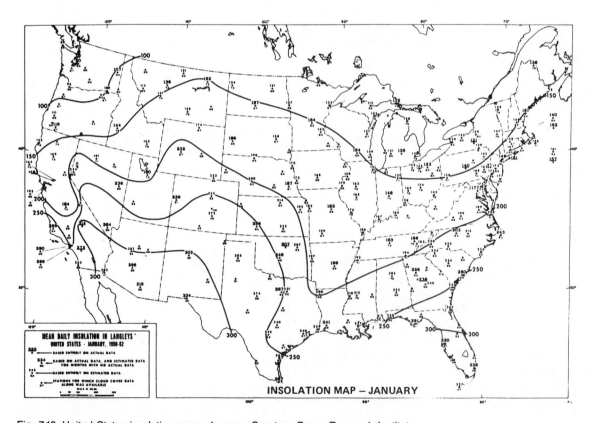

Fig. 7-18. United States insolation map—January. Courtesy Brace Research Institute.

concentrations. If the sunlight comes into the atmosphere at an angle, it has to go through more air (and dust, etc.) than if it enters directly overhead. Measurements in a city may be as much as 15 to 20 percent lower than values in the surrounding countryside. Hence, measurements in a city may not be applicable to the suburbs or countryside, and vice versa.

There are several good compilations of solar energy input. Figures 7-18 and 7-19 illustrate insolation maps for the United States for two months of the "typical" year. While certainly not completely accurate, they will help the swimming pool solar panel builder in deciding how much sun arrives at his location.

The units in the maps are given in *Langleys* per day. A Langley equals 1 gram-calorie/square centimeter or 3.69 BTU/square foot. Here's how to convert Langleys per day to BTU per square foot per day:

Langleys/day	BTU/sq. ft. day
100	369
150	554
200	738
250	922
300	1100
350	1290
400	1475
450	1660
500	1845
550	2130
600	2220
650	2400
700	2580
750	2760

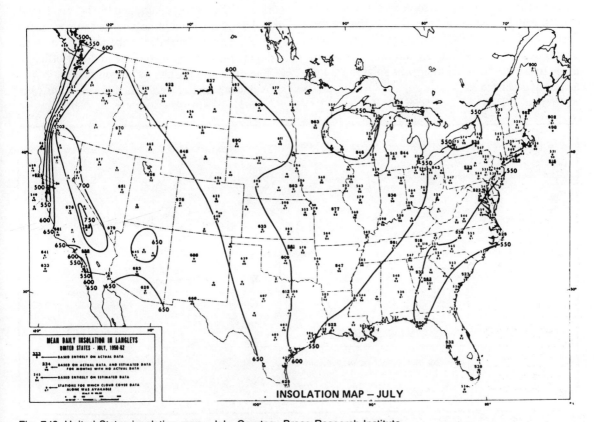

INSOLATION MAP – JULY

Fig. 7-19. United States insolation map—July. Courtesy Brace Research Institute.

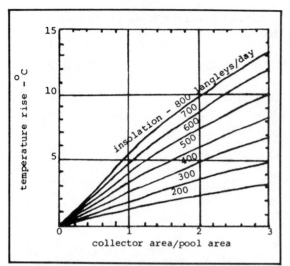

Fig. 7-20. Graph for planning swimming pool collector area. Courtesy U.S. Department of Energy.

The time of day will also dictate the amount of solar energy your geographical location receives. There are many variables in the planning of a solar pool (Fig. 7-20), but enough generalizations can be made to use useful in building your solar hot water heater and collectors.

SOLAR WATER HEATER SYSTEMS

Two types of solar heaters (Figs. 7-21 to 7-23) can be made using this chapter: one is also a roof cover with full weatherproofing properties, the other is only a solar heater. Both feature an inlet and an outlet manifold which are plumbed into the pool recirculation system. The inlet and outlet manifolds are connected by many small tubes which are in turn soldered to copper sheet. The sheet intercepts and collects the solar energy and conducts it to the tubes where it is carried off by the water.

For a heater which is also a roof, it's best to use the 16-ounce or 20-ounce copper sheet. For a solar heat collector only, any thickness of copper sheet is acceptable, but the 10-ounce material will be less expensive than the thicker ones.

There is also an optimum spacing for the tubes soldered to the sheet. If the spacing is too large, the sheet between the tubes gets too hot, too much heat gets lost to the surroundings, and the heat collected per dollar of investment suffers. If the spacing is too small, the sheet metal is not being made to work hard enough, and again you lose in dollar efficiency. The optimum spacing is shown in Fig. 7-24.

It doesn't matter very much if you build your

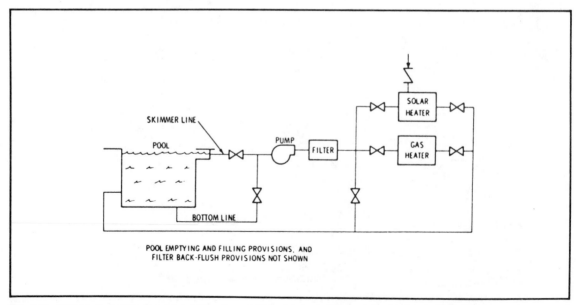

Fig. 7-21. Plumbing diagram involving both solar and gas heaters. Courtesy Brace Research Institute.

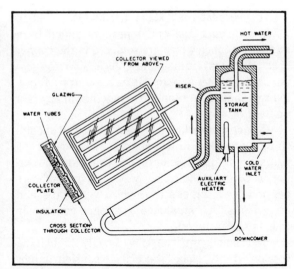

Fig. 7-22. Detailed view of a typical solar collector and storage tank. Courtesy National Science Foundation.

collector with a spacing an inch or two off optimum. The cost effectiveness will not change very much. Most collectors for heating swimming pools should be of the "unglazed" type.

COLLECTOR GUIDELINES

Here are some simple design guidelines for designing your own solar pool heating and collecting system.

If you have a small or medium size pool, use 1 1/2-inch tubing for the plumbing. If the pool is large, use 2-inch tubing. With thin sheet material, you might use a spacing of 8 inches, for thick material either 8 or 10 inches depending on the width of the sheet material you are able to buy. Use tubes of 3/8-inch nominal diameter. Don't use less than about ten heater tubes in parallel. If you use relatively few, use 1/2-inch tubing. If you use about 15 tubes or more you might use 3/8 inch.

On a combination heater/roof the length of the tubes should not be more than about 30 feet. On a heater which doesn't have the roofing function, you can build it longer if you wish, but you should allow for thermal expansion.

THE SOLAR COLLECTOR

A solar collector with no roofing function can

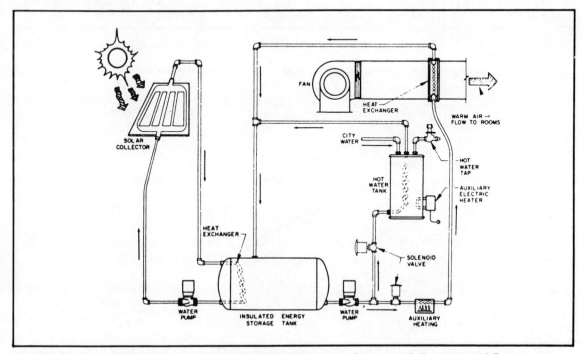

Fig. 7-23. Schematic diagram of a solar heating and hot water system. Courtesy U.S. Department of Energy.

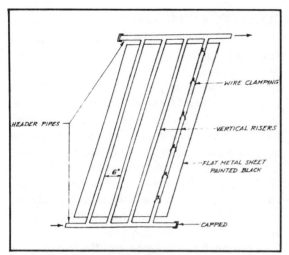

Fig. 7-24. Optimum spacing of solar collector vertical risers. Courtesy Brace Research Institute.

A solar heater will look much like Figs. 7-25 to 7-27, with inlet and outlet headers joined by a number of tubes which are soldered to the copper sheet. There is one major difference. Since the copper sheet doesn't have to also be a waterproof roofing membrane, you can put it together in any of a number of ways.

The collector should be held down well enough so that a windstorm will not cause damage. If it's necessary to make penetrations through the roofing or roofing shingles, it's best to use barbed copper or bronze nails or screws which will not rust and cause leaks. Sealant should be applied generously around the fasteners.

You shouldn't nail or screw directly through the copper sheet, since thermal expansion might enlarge the holes or loosen the fasteners. It's probably best to use some cleating arrangement or a copper strap or a strong wire stretched over the tubes. If you live in an area where there is frequent and serious damage caused by windstorms, the heater strips should be held down about every 18 inches. If you live in a calm area, you might use a hold-down spacing of 3 feet. There should be a sup-

be mounted on any smooth surface which has an acceptable orientation and is not shaded. This may be on a roof, on a covered patio area, on any platform, on a hillside, or in an unused portion of a garden where the collector can be tied down and nothing will grow to shade it.

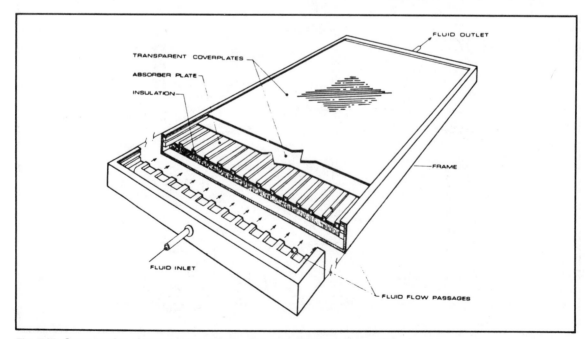

Fig. 7-25. Cross section of typical solar collector. Courtesy U.S. Department of Energy.

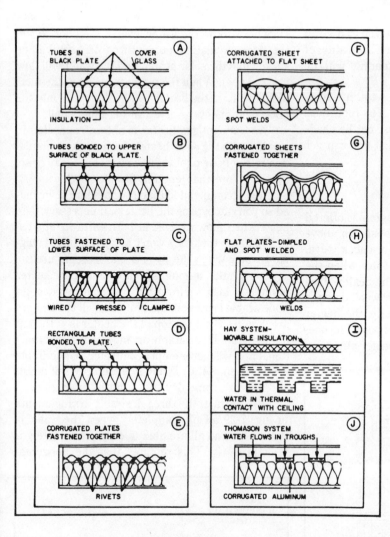

Fig. 7-26. Cross section of collectors for water heaters. Courtesy of National Science Foundation.

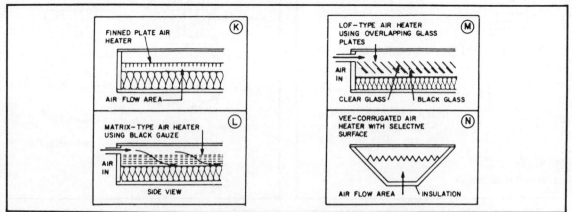

Fig. 7-27. Cross section of collectors for air heaters. Courtesy National Science Foundation.

port close to the manifolds so that you can strap them down to the support structure. Fabrication of manifolds, soldering, and final coating will be discussed later in this chapter.

A solar collector which will also fulfill a roofing function can be built on a roof. The roof must have an acceptable orientation, must not be shaded, and have a sufficient area so that you can get the pool heating effect you want.

PLUMBING

A typical solar heater piping diagram is offered in Fig. 7-28. The reversed-Z symbol shown above the solar heater is a one-way valve or check valve. Its purpose is to empty the solar heater when the pump is not on by letting air into the heater. This valve is installed so freezing weather won't damage the heater. For this to work properly, the heater should be above the water level of the pool. The one-way valve can be hooked into the heater plumbing

anywhere above the water level of the pool. When the pool circulation pump turns off, air will be sucked into the solar heater, and the water will flow into the pool. When the pump turns on in the morning, the air in the heater will be "burped" into the pool. The one-way valve can be quite small.

An optional gas heater is shown connected in parallel with the solar heater. With modern circulation rates of one pool volume every ten hours or so, there is more than enough flow for both.

It is recommended that a bypass line be included so you can bypass the heaters, if necessary. The heaters are shown valved at both entrance and exit. This is so that they won't be forced full of stagnant water when the bypass line is being used.

Let's take a look at good and bad heater plumbing logic. First, Fig. 7-28 illustrates an undesirable arrangement. Note that all the heaters are drawn so that the top of the heater is at the top of the figure. Undesirable arrangement B will function, but it will never empty completely. Undesirable arrangements A, C, D, and E will empty, but might end up with some dry tubes during operation.

By contrast, the three desirable arrangements in Fig. 7-29 all fill completely when the water is turned on, and all are able to empty completely if built properly. This requires that the horizontal

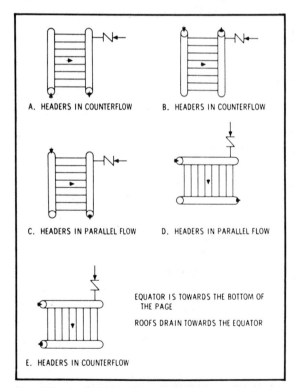

Fig. 7-28. Undesirable heater plumbing arrangements. Courtesy Brace Research Institute.

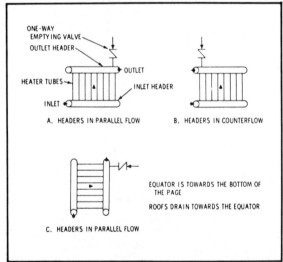

Fig. 7-29. Desirable heater plumbing arrangements. Courtesy Brace Research Institute.

tubes in the design, if tilted at all, be tilted in the right direction. For example, in *A* and *B* the manifolds or headers are normally horizontal. Both inlet and outlet headers should be able to drain completely by being tilted slightly so that the water will flow in the proper direction. In *C* the heater tubes are nominally horizontal. They should be tilted slightly so that the water can flow towards the inlet header. The lower part of the outlet header is shown as a dead end which will stay filled with water when the pump is turned off. This dead-end section should be as short as possible.

ASSEMBLY

When assembling the plumbing, the importance of planning the plumbing diagram (Fig. 7-3), determining the required tube lengths, and careful measuring and cutting cannot be stressed too much. In planning the plumbing layout, make sure that you allow for thermal expansion. It's best not to have a straight tube rigidly tied to something at both ends, especially if the tube is long. When the temperature of the tube changes, the ends will want to push out or pull in. If they are restrained, stresses will be imposed on the tube and the joints. In addition, horizontal tubing should be supported at least every 8 feet.

In measuring the tube you will need to take into account the length taken up by the fittings. A tube cutter is best for cutting the tube. You can also use a hacksaw, especially for large tubing. A miter box is useful. All burrs and slivers must be removed before making any tubing joints, whether you use soldered or flared joints. Copper tubing can be readily bent with a tube bender. For tubing larger than 1 inch in diameter, it's better to use fittings than make a bend.

SOLDERING

Solders are highly specialized alloys, the most common ones consisting of tin and lead. For copper tubing and sheeting, the best solder is 50A solder, composed of 50 percent tin and 50 percent lead. This composition will melt completely at a relatively low soldering temperature, has very good wetting and capillary action, and produces good reliable joints.

The most convenient solder for the tubing is the round wire type, 1/8-inch diameter with no flux core. The flux should be bought separately. For soldering tubes to the sheet, the 1/8-inch solder is thin and should be twisted together in a three-strand or four-strand solder rope for convenience.

A flux is used for most soldering operations to facilitate the soldering process by performing a number of tasks. The surfaces should be clean before the flux is applied. Then the flux can dissolve any oxide layer or other dirt which still might be on the surface. If a perfectly clean surface were heated without flux, the oxide layer formed by the time the surface got to soldering temperature would make the soldering process difficult. The flux protects the surface from oxygen as well as dissolving any oxide layer. The flux helps the solder wet the metal and is displaced by the solder.

For soldering copper a number of fluxes are acceptable. There are paste fluxes made of petroleum jelly and zinc chloride. They are quite inexpensive and effective.

SOLDERING TECHNIQUES

Copper tubing and sheeting are soldered with "soldering coppers." A torch can be used, but care must be taken not to overheat the work with a large torch. Overheating may burn the flux, making it necessary to clean the material again, flux again, and solder again.

A small torch may not have the capacity to do the job. A large propane, butane, or gasoline torch, or an air-acetylene or oxyacetylene torch should be used. Be careful not to overheat the work if you use a large torch.

Heat both parts being soldered and avoid keeping the torch in one spot for a long time. A sweeping motion is best. You can feed the solder into the flame area intermittently. Then "draw" it along with the flame until more is needed.

Before starting on either the tube-to-sheet soldering, or the sheet metal work, it's best to practice on some pieces of scrap. It's essential to keep the tube from shifting while the solder is solidify-

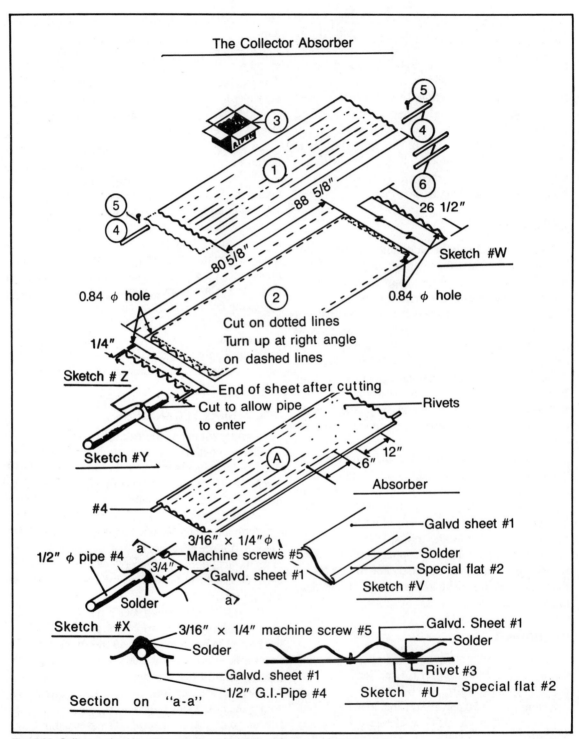

The Collector Absorber

88 5/8"

80 5/8"

26 1/2"

Sketch #W

5 4 6

0.84 φ hole

1/4"

Sketch # Z

0.84 φ hole

(2) Cut on dotted lines
Turn up at right angle
on dashed lines

End of sheet after cutting
Cut to allow pipe
to enter

Rivets

Sketch #Y

(A)

12"

6"

#4

Absorber

Galvd sheet #1

3/16" × 1/4" φ
Machine screws #5

1/2" φ pipe #4

3/4"

Galvd. sheet #1

Solder

Solder
Special flat #2

Sketch #V

Sketch #X

3/16" × 1/4" machine screw #5

Galvd. Sheet #1

Solder

Galvd. sheet #1

1/2" G.I.-Pipe #4

Section on "a-a"

Rivet #3

Special flat #2

Sketch #U

Fig. 7-30. Collector plumbing diagram. Courtesy Brace Research Institute.

ing. If the tubing moves, the solder may crack, and much of the heat transfer effectiveness of the solder bond may be lost.

On a roof/heater put in two or three tubes first, then put in the finished manifolds using these tubes as support. Put in the other tubes, first soldering them to the manifolds and tacking them down every 2 feet or so before you start soldering. The tubing tends to expand in the soldering operation. Tack it down first at the two ends, then in the middle, then in the middle of the two halves, etc. This will minimize waviness in the final product.

When soldering tubes on a roofing heater, it's important to avoid overheating the sealant used on the nearer battens. You might use a wet towel draped over the batten next to the tubing you are soldering to the roof. Or, you might solder the tubes on first, and then put on the sealant and the batten caps.

A heater which doesn't have a roofing function can be made in parts. Then it is assembled without the sectional tacking described previously.

When soldering on a steep slope, paste flux may be best. Otherwise, a water-based flux is recommended. It is much easier to clean off after the soldering operation.

Flux should be applied no more than an hour before soldering. It shouldn't be left on overnight since it will make soldering more difficult.

SOLAR COLLECTOR COATINGS

Much research and development has been done on coatings for solar collectors (Fig. 7-31). The search has been for an ideal "selective absorber," which will absorb close to 100 percent of the incoming sunlight, but will radiate as little as possible of the energy back to the surroundings. The coating should be inexpensive on a square foot basis and should have a long useful life.

Better than black paint are coatings such as Sears, Roebuck and Company's "Tar Emulsion Driveway Coating and Sealer," manufactured by Chevron Asphalt Company. It's easy to apply without a primer coat, has good solar absorption qualities which don't change rapidly, and can easi-

ly be renewed if necessary after a few years. Similar coatings are available in other brands.

If you plan to use a glazed or glass-covered collector, don't use a tar coating. It will evaporate partially in service, coating the glass and reducing efficiency. Instead, use a black paint and primer combination that can be applied on copper.

For application, the surfaces should be cleaned thoroughly. Paste flux should be cleaned off with an organic solvent. The coating and sealer should then be applied in two coats, following the instructions. It can best be done with a common paint brush such as a 4-inch brush. It's best to apply the coating during the morning and give it a full day of drying time before there is a chance to condense dew on the coating.

If the coating gets very dusty in service, it can be hosed down occasionally. If it should become desirable to renew the coating, the surface should be rubbed down thoroughly with an abrasive household cleaner, and then hosed and brushed off well, before it is recoated.

COLLECTOR MAINTENANCE

The collector should be hosed down every now and then to remove accumulated dirt. Bird droppings should not be left on indefinitely, since they tend to make the coating peel. Every few months or so the collector might be left turned off for a full (hot) day so that any moisture which may have accumulated on the roofing, has a chance to evaporate. If the roof is always cooled by the solar heater during the daytime, condensed moisture might accumulate. Every few years, when it becomes apparent that the coating is either beginning to get thin or to lighten appreciably, the surface can be recoated as described earlier.

The filter should be cleaned regularly so that the solar heater gets a high enough water flow rate.

SOLAR POOL COVERS

One of the easiest and least expensive ways of increasing the temperature of pool water is to cover it with a sheet of clear plastic. If the pool is located in a sunny spot, it becomes a heat collector.

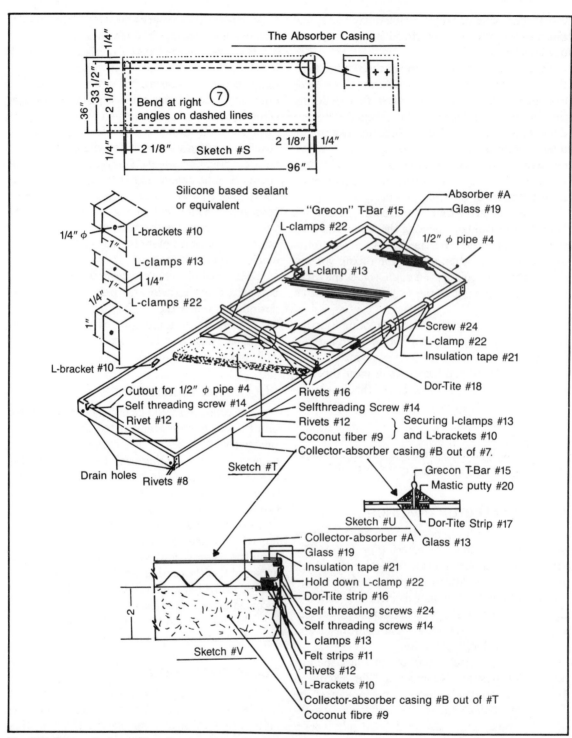

The Absorber Casing

1/4"
33 1/2"
36"
2 1/8"

Bend at right
angles on dashed lines

⑦

Sketch #S

2 1/8"

2 1/8"

1/4"

1/4"

96"

Silicone based sealant
or equivalent

1/4" φ

L-brackets #10

1"

L-clamps #13

1/4"

1"

L-clamps #22

1/4"

1"

L-bracket #10

"Grecon" T-Bar #15

L-clamps #22

L-clamp #13

Absorber #A

Glass #19

1/2" φ pipe #4

Screw #24

L-clamp #22

Insulation tape #21

Cutout for 1/2" φ pipe #4

Self threading screw #14

Rivet #12

Drain holes

Rivets #8

Rivets #16

Selfthreading Screw #14

Rivets #12

Coconut fiber #9

Collector-absorber casing #B out of #7.

Dor-Tite #18

} Securing I-clamps #13
and L-brackets #10

Sketch #T

Grecon T-Bar #15

Mastic putty #20

Sketch #U

Dor-Tite Strip #17

Glass #13

Collector-absorber #A

Glass #19

Insulation tape #21

Hold down L-clamp #22

Dor-Tite strip #16

Self threading screws #24

Self threading screws #14

L clamps #13

Felt strips #11

Rivets #12

L-Brackets #10

Collector-absorber casing #B out of #T

Coconut fibre #9

2

Sketch #V

Fig. 7-31. Solar collector coating. Courtesy Brace Research Institute.

Even if it is located in the shade, the cover reduces heat losses, especially evaporative losses. In a sunny location, a plastic covered swimming pool will be about 10° F. warmer than an uncovered pool.

Pool covers can be either transparent or opaque. Transparent covers allow solar energy to penetrate deeply into the pool, warming the water. About 75 percent of the sun's energy that penetrates the cover will warm the pool. Also, nighttime radiation losses are slightly less from a transparent cover than those from an uncovered pool. The most popular transparent pool covers are of clear polypropylene, polyethylene, or vinyl of four to six-mil thickness. They may be purchased inexpensively at most hardware and building supply stores.

Light colored opaque covers drastically reduce the sunlight warming the pool and so are best for use as nighttime covers. Dark or black opaque covers will hold pool heat in, but don't allow sunlight to heat the water so they only warm the top few inches of pool water. They are also less effective at night.

There are also liquid chemical evaporation retardants. These easily spread and cover the surface of the pool with an extremely thin evaporation retarding film.

Swimming pool covers can also have a secondary purpose of increasing safety. With a frame or anchors, the cover can keep children and objects from falling into the pool when not in use. The cover should be of a stronger fabric that can withstand heavier weights and punctures.

For safety, *always* remove the *entire* pool cover whenever anyone is swimming. Otherwise a disoriented swimmer may swim under the cover and become trapped.

Chapter 8

Pool Structures and Landscaping

Once your swimming pool is installed, there are many things you can do in your yard to improve its use. You can add an enclosure, build a fence, install a deck, and plan landscaping. All these topics and more will be covered in this chapter.

The first step in deciding what pool structures and landscaping to install is to decide how much and when you will use your pool. If you decide to use it year round, you will probably need to build an enclosure (Fig. 8-1). If your pool is as much for beauty as for function, landscaping will be important. If your large family enjoys lying about in the sun around your above-ground pool, a deck will be vital. If you live in an area where privacy or security is important, a fence will be necessary (Fig. 8-2).

Another primary consideration is money. How much do you have left in your "swimming pool budget" once you've installed your pool? While it's a good idea to set some money aside for structures and landscaping, things seem to always cost more than you had planned. The later elements often die for lack of funding. Let's consider how you can get the most for your pool dollar with pool enclosures, structures, and landscaping.

POOL ENCLOSURES

Swimming pool enclosures offer many advantages over an uncovered pool. First, they are often designed as excellent solar collectors, allowing the sun to warm the trapped air within the enclosure as well as the water in the pool. It also conserves heat by holding it in day and night. A pool enclosure offers safety and protection by keeping children and animals out of the pool. It also excludes pesky insects, dust, and falling leaves, making pool maintenance a simpler chore. Best of all, a pool enclosure allows swimming in any weather. Heat from the pool heats the enclosure for comfort and allows swimming day or night, fall and spring.

Swimming pool enclosures (Figs. 8-3 and 8-4) come in all sizes, shapes, and designs, including rectangular, square, shed-type, and cylindrical. The most popular is the rectangular-shaped enclosure.

Fig. 8-1. A table by the pool is a good place to relax. Courtesy Richardson Industries, Inc.

Fig. 8-2. A fence is important to pool privacy and security. Courtesy Koppers Co., Inc.

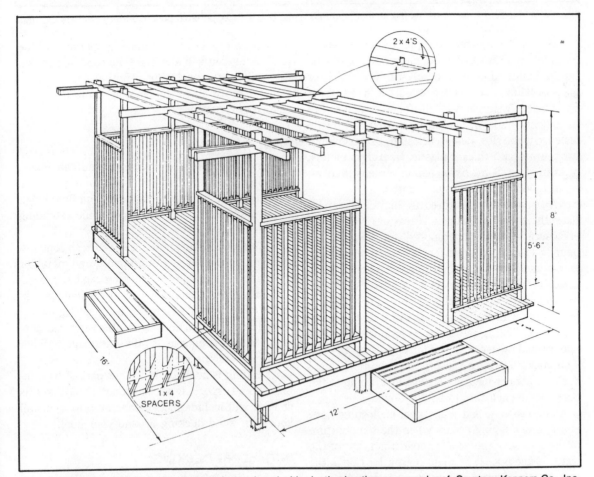

Fig. 8-3. Frame for pool enclosure that can be enclosed with plastic sheeting or a wood roof. Courtesy Koppers Co., Inc.

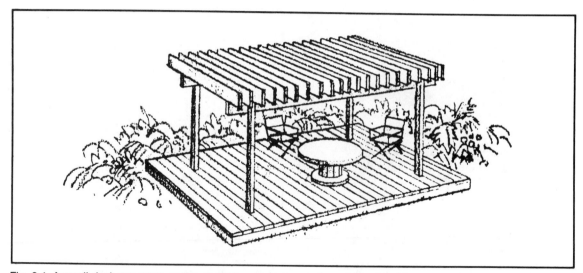

Fig. 8-4. A small deck can serve as the shaded summer home of a smaller portable pool. Courtesy Koppers Co., Inc.

Pool enclosures can be supported in two ways: frame or air. Frames of wood, aluminum, or plastic can be built and covered by plastic, fiberglass, or glass paneling. Many pool enclosure kits can be set up in a day. A simple wooden ribbed structure can be quickly built with clear polyethylene plastic fastened to the ribs. Better enclosures use aluminum framework with thicker plastic, fiberglass panels, or even glass. Some have snap-in screens that can be installed during warmer months.

Air-supported structures use blower fans to inflate them like a balloon. Pressure within the enclosure should be produced for about 1000 pounds of air per cubic foot of space within the enclosure. Reinforcement strips are sometimes sewn across the seams in lieu of inside framework. In sizing an air-supported pool enclosure, add at least 6 feet to the width of your pool and 8 to 12 feet to the length. That is, the enclosure for a 16-by-32-foot pool should measure approximately 22 by 44 feet. The enclosure can be secured by traditional pool deck anchors or by using water-filled tubing at the base of the enclosure to hold it down.

One problem that many pool enclosures have is fogging. Fogging occurs when the temperature of the air above the pool is cooler than that of the water in the pool. The main reason for this is the lack of an air heater within the enclosure. By war-

ming the air to the approximate temperature of the pool water, you will eliminate the condensation on the walls of the enclosure. Another solution is to vent the moist air to the outside before it has the chance to condense.

POOL DECKING

One of the best investments you can make, dollar for dollar, around your swimming pool is in decking. Decking is both beautiful and functional. If can make your pool look larger while extending its usefulness.

Most swimming pools are edged with coping—stone in the case of in-ground pools, and metal for most above-ground pools. Decking can begin within a couple feet of this coping or even come up right to the edge of your swimming pool, saving money in some cases. Wood decking is often safer than concrete or rock coping as it offers drainage without a slick and slippery finish.

Decking is such an important part of both in-ground and especially above-ground pools that this chapter will include instructions on how to install your own wood decking around your pool.

INSTALLING DECKING

The first thing to consider in planning and installing pool decking is materials. Since the decking will be subjected to man's and nature's worst elements—bleach and the sun—it should be a type that will withstand the effects as long as possible. Redwood and cedar are good natural choices for pool decking. Another is pressure-treated lumber, such as Wolmanized® lumber available at many building material yards.

The location and design of your deck should be influenced by several factors: anticipated use, air currents, height and size of the pool, whether it's an in-ground or above-ground pool, other existing structures, privacy, view, safety, access to home, terrain, and other personal preferences. You should also consider whether to plan for building a pool enclosure on top of it. If so, you will want to stress it for the additional weight.

Make sure that the deck doesn't seal access to any utility or drainage lines. If you aren't sure of the location or depth of buried electric, telephone, gas, water, or sewer lines, it's a good idea to ask your utilities.

In sizing your deck, keep in mind its intended use. Will it accommodate benches, lounge chairs, perhaps a table for outdoor dining? How many may sunbathe? How will it blend in with your pool and/or coping?

Once you've decided on the basic size, shape, and location of your deck, check local building codes. A construction permit for your swimming pool may also be written to cover your deck and any related structures.

DECK DESIGN

Decks (Fig. 8-5) consist of six parts: footings, posts, beams, joists, decking, and railings. In planning for these, you have three basic considerations: function, structural stability, and appearance.

The aesthetics of your pool deck will probably be most noticeable in your choice of railing and decking. The location of posts and beams, however, can have a major effect on the appearance of a raised deck. In almost every instance, your choice lies between several small pieces of lumber or comparatively fewer large ones. A railing, for example,

may be held by 2-×-4-foot posts spaced every 16 inches or less, or it may have 4-×-4-foot posts capped by a 2 × 6 spaced as far apart as 8 feet. Your best guide at this stage is to look at various swimming pool deck plans and inspect decks completed by friends and neighbors to help you decide what you like best.

As an example of how to design and build your own swimming pool deck, we'll use a deck attached to a house on one side. This type is most popular with above-ground pools. Refer to Fig. 8-6. The outside edge can be shaped if adjacent to the rounded end of your pool.

Let's say that your deck will extend 8 feet from the house and be 14 feet long. If it's to be just above ground level, there's little need for a railing. Higher decks, however, call for a sturdy railing using 4 × 4 posts or something comparable.

Table 8-1 shows the appropriate beam size. For example, the distance between the house and the beam is 8 feet. A 4-×-8 foot beam allows a span of 7 feet between posts, a convenient figure for a deck 14 feet long. A beam can be a single piece of the dimension specified (Table 8-2), or built up from two smaller pieces either nailed together or placed a few inches apart on either side of a post.

To calculate the size post needed, multiply the beam spacing (8 feet in this case) by the post spacing (7 feet). This gives you the load area: 56 square feet. Table 8-3 shows that for a load area less than 72 square feet and a post height under 6 feet, a 4-×-4-foot post is adequate.

Decking in this example will be 2-×-6-foot boards, laid flat. Table 8-4 shows the safe spans for decking.

Now refer to Table 8-5. As in the example, joists must span the 8 feet between the house and the outer beam. That can be achieved with 2-×-8-foot joists spaced 32 inches apart. The 32-inch spacing is within the maximum span of 48 inches allowable for the 2-×-6-foot decking.

If you are building a self-supporting deck around the perimeter of your pool, you will have some portions not anchored to the side of the house. This free-standing decking will require additional posts based on the same design concepts.

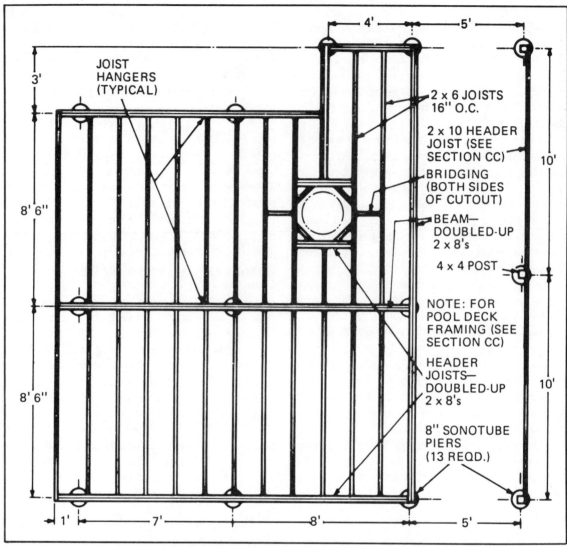

JOIST HANGERS (TYPICAL)

3'

8' 6"

8' 6"

1'

7'

8'

5'

4'

5'

2 x 6 JOISTS 16" O.C.

2 x 10 HEADER JOIST (SEE SECTION CC)

BRIDGING (BOTH SIDES OF CUTOUT)

BEAM— DOUBLED-UP 2 x 8's

4 x 4 POST

NOTE: FOR POOL DECK FRAMING (SEE SECTION CC)

HEADER JOISTS— DOUBLED-UP 2 x 8's

8" SONOTUBE PIERS (13 REQD.)

10'

10'

Fig. 8-5. Layout of typical deck. Courtesy Western Wood Products Assn.

INSTALLATION PROCEDURES

The first step in installing your swimming pool decking is to mark off the deck area using string and batter boards (Fig. 8-7), making sure that it is level and square. The string will help you visualize the size and appearance of the finished deck and will also serve as a guide for excavation and post placement.

Step 2 includes preparing the site. With a spade or sod cutter, remove the sod to a depth of 2 or 3

inches. Uncover an area approximately 2 feet larger than the planned deck. It's unlikely that grass will be able to grow in the shadow of your deck, so you might as well transfer the sod to a bare spot in your yard where it will be useful.

Next, locate and dig holes for footings. In normal soil the holes should be a minimum of 24 inches deep, although the actual depth will depend on the height of the column and depth of the frost line. Posts should go deeper than the frost line to

110

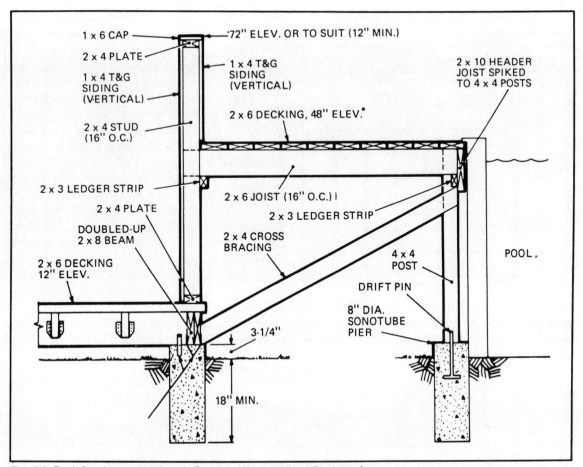

Fig. 8-6. Deck for above-ground pool. Courtesy Western Wood Products Assn.

Table 8-1. Minimum Beam Sizes. Courtesy Koppers Co., Inc.

Length of Span (ft.)	Spacing between beams (ft.)						
	4	5	6	7	8	9	10
6	4 x 6	4 x 6	4 x 6	4 x 8	4 x 8	4 x 8	4 x 10
7	4 x 8	4 x 8	4 x 8	4 x 8	4 x 8	4 x 10	4 x 10
8	4 x 8	4 x 8	4 x 8	4 x 10	4 x 10	4 x 10	4 x 12
9	4 x 8	4 x 8	4 x 10	4 x 10	4 x 10	4 x 12	*
10	4 x 8	4 x 10	4 x 10	4 x 12	4 x 12	*	*
11	4 x 10	4 x 10	4 x 12	4 x 12	*	*	*
12	4 x 10	4 x 12	4 x 12	4 x 12	*	*	*

*Beams larger than 4 x 12 recommended. Consult a designer for appropriate sizes.

Lumber Dimensions

Nominal (inches)	Dry (inches)
1	3/4
2	1½
4	3½
6	5½
8	7¼
10	9¼
12	11¼

avoid heaving during freeze and thaw cycles. Refer to Fig. 8-8. In the bottom of the holes place a 6-inch layer of gravel and tamp firm, or pour a 3-inch con-crete footing and top it with gravel to allow for drain-age. Upright posts can then be positioned in this base (Fig. 8-9).

Now secure beams to posts. Using a string and level, find the desired deck height on the posts. By subtracting the actual thickness of the deck board, joist, and beam, you'll have determined the correct spot for the bottom side of the beam. Cut the post at that point and fasten the beam on top by one of the methods illustrated in Fig. 8-9.

Step 5: Attach joists to the house and beams as illustrated in Figs. 8-10, 8-11, and 8-12. If you're building a free-standing deck, you'll simply repeat the previous step on this side of the deck. Joists are attached to the house with joists hangers or sup-ported by a ledger strip. The placement of the ledger determines the level of the deck floor, so be sure it is positioned at the correct height and is horizontal.

If you've planned railing, install the posts now as shown in Fig. 8-13. These can be a continuation

Table 8-3. Minimum Post Sizes. Courtesy Koppers Co., Inc.

Height (ft.)	Load area (sq. ft.) = beam spacing x post spacing				
	48	72	96	120	144
Up to 6	4 x 4	4 x 4	6 x 6	6 x 6	6 x 6
Up to 9	6 x 6	6 x 6	6 x 6	6 x 6	6 x 6

Vertical loads figured as concentric along post axis. No lateral loads considered.

Table 8-4. Maximum Allowable Spans for Spaced Deck Boards. Courtesy Koppers Co., Inc.

Maximum allowable span (inches)		
Laid flat		Laid on edge
2 x 4 32	2 x 6 48	2 x 4 96

Though able to support greater spans, the maximum spans will result in undersirable deflection or springiness in a deck.

Table 8-5. Maximum Allowable Spans for Deck Joists. Courtesy Koppers Co., Inc.

Joist size (inches)	Joist spacing (inches)		
	16	24	32
2 x 6	9'-9"	7'-11"	6'-2"
2 x 8		10'-6"	8'-1"
2 x 10	16'-5"	13'-4"	10'-4"

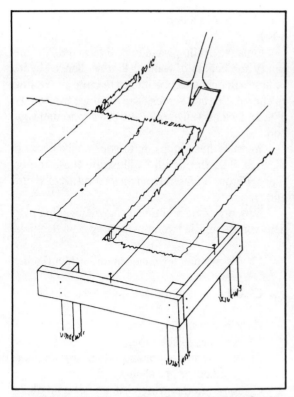

Fig. 8-7. Batterboards and string. Courtesy Koppers Co., Inc.

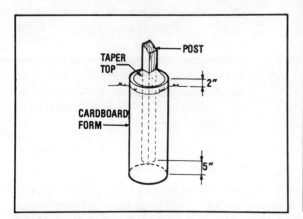

Fig. 8-8. Posts should go deeper than the frost line. Courtesy Georgia-Pacific Corp.

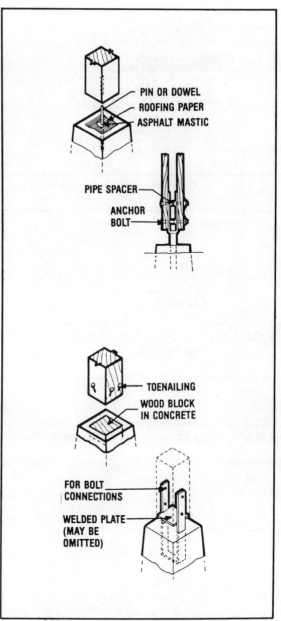

Fig. 8-9. Upright posts can be attached to footing blocks. Courtesy Georgia-Pacific Corp.

of the posts which support the deck, or railing posts may be bolted to the outside joist or joist extensions. Refer also to Fig. 8-14.

Next, install deck boards using hot-dipped, galvanized-coated, 12-penny (12d) nails such as those in Fig. 8-15. (Refer to Fig. 8-16 for a popular decking design.) Separate 1/4 to 1/2 inch to allow for expansion and contraction. This can be done quickly by using a spacer as in Fig. 8-17. If you install decking using straight planking, you can trim

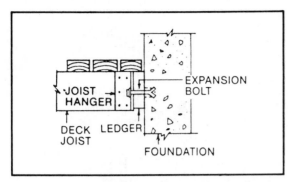

Fig. 8-10. Using a joist hanger. Courtesy Koppers Co., Inc.

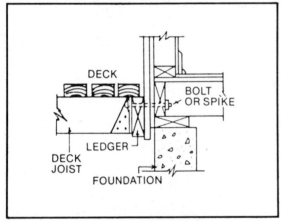

Fig. 8-11. Using a bolt or spike. Courtesy Koppers Co., Inc.

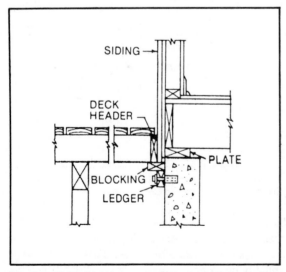

Fig. 8-12. Using blocking to attach the deck. Courtesy Koppers Co., Inc.

your deck after nailing to assure a straight line (Fig. 8-18).

Finish the railing as in Figs. 8-19 and 8-20. The safety and beauty of your deck are enhanced by its railings. Benches can be integrated into the railing as shown. Privacy screens can enhance the beauty of your deck as well as offer you privacy around your pool.

You may need steps up to your pool's deck. If so, Figs. 8-21 through 8-24 illustrate the common types. Figure 8-25 offers suggested ratios of risers and treads.

Here are some additional suggestions that may help you in building your swimming pool decking.

- ☐ Always nail a thinner member to a thicker member.
- ☐ Drive nails at a slight angle toward each other for greater holding power.
- ☐ When toenailing, stagger opposing nails so they pass each other.
- ☐ For maximum holding power, use angular-shanked or spiral-shanked nails.
- ☐ To reduce splitting, drill a pilot hold about three-quarters of the diameter of the nail.
- ☐ Place nails no closer to the edge than about half the board thickness and no closer to the end than the thickness of the board. When nailing closer to an edge, predrill the holes.
- ☐ Tops of upright structures and joist ends should be beveled to a 30-degree to 45-degree angle for drainage to minimize moisture absorption.

PLANNING A POOL FENCE

A fence can be an excellent addition to your swimming pool area offering privacy, security, and function. Your fence can reduce or eliminate the view of the pool from the outside. It can insure that children and pets are not allowed in the pool area without supervision. A fence can also serve as a buffer against the elements, reducing wind chill or offering shade.

Your fence can be of a number of materials. The most popular are wood and chain link which we'll

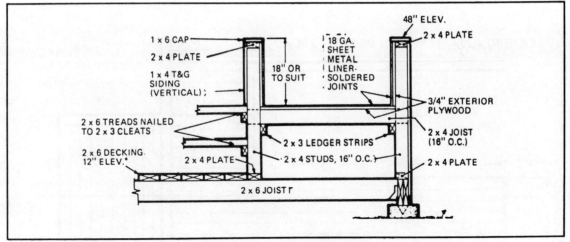

Fig. 8-13. Installing posts for railings. Courtesy Western Wood Products Assn.

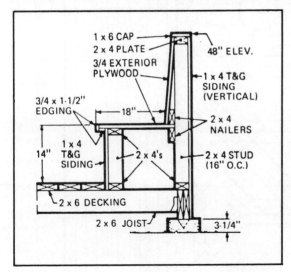

Fig. 8-14. Building a deck bench. Courtesy Western Wood Products Assn.

discuss here. For a more comprehensive look at all types of fences and related structures, refer to my book *The Complete Book of Fences* (TAB Book No. 1508).

Before you begin building your fence, be sure to check local building codes for regulations on fence height and location. Go over property lines carefully. You might discuss a common ownership of the fence with your neighbor. Study the prevailing wind patterns and allow for them in your planning. You may want to deflect the wind or take advantage of breezes.

To assure lifetime service, your best bet for posts—which of course come in direct contact with the ground—is the heartwood of cedar or pressure-treated posts of most other species. The little added cost will pay you well. If not available, ask your dealer for installation recommendations that have

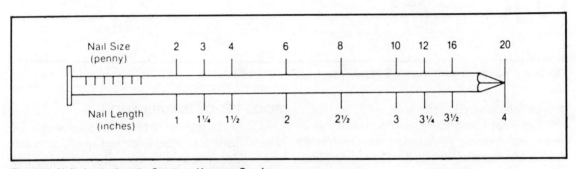

Fig. 8-15. Nail size by length. Courtesy Koppers Co., Inc.

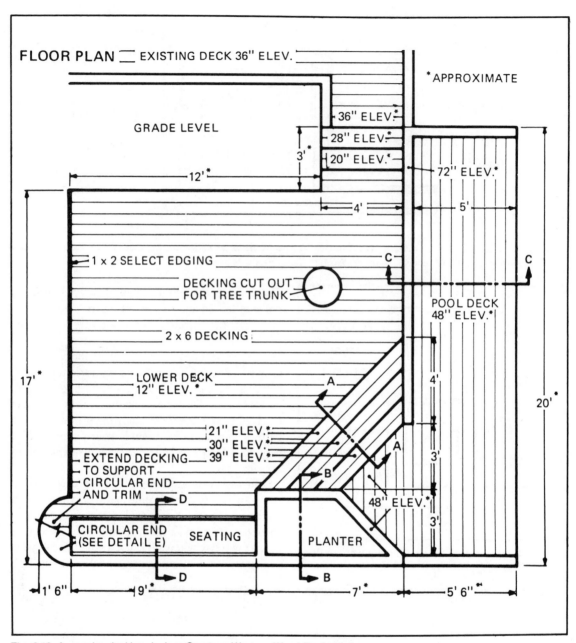

FLOOR PLAN — EXISTING DECK 36" ELEV.

*APPROXIMATE

GRADE LEVEL

36" ELEV.*
28" ELEV.*
3'*
20" ELEV.*
72" ELEV.*

12'*

4'

5'

1 x 2 SELECT EDGING

C

C

DECKING CUT OUT
FOR TREE TRUNK

POOL DECK
48" ELEV.*

2 x 6 DECKING

LOWER DECK
12" ELEV. *

17'*

A

4'

20'*

21" ELEV.*
30" ELEV.*
39" ELEV.*

A

3'

EXTEND DECKING
TO SUPPORT
CIRCULAR END
AND TRIM

B

48" ELEV.*

D

3'

CIRCULAR END
(SEE DETAIL E)

SEATING

PLANTER

D

B

1' 6"

9'*

7'*

5' 6"*

Fig. 8-16. A popular decking design. Courtesy Western Wood Products Assn.

proven satisfactory in your area.

For fence construction, you'll probably want posts and framing in *Standard* or *Construction* grades. Board grades include the *Commons* for knotty appearance and the *Selects* for clearer stock.

POOL FENCE INSTALLATION

To begin, use string to outline your area to be fenced. Locate the holes 4 to 8 feet apart depending upon which design you're using. Dig each hole 3 feet deep, then place 2 inches of gravel on the bottom.

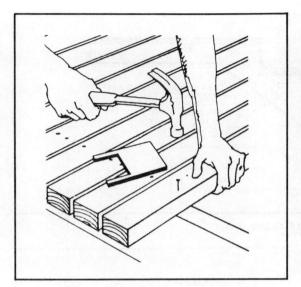

Fig. 8-17. Using a spacer. Courtesy Koppers Co., Inc.

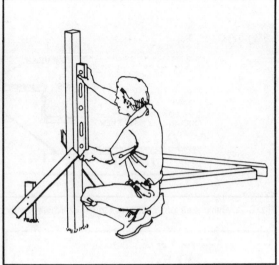

Fig. 8-19. Adding a post for the railing. Courtesy Koppers Co., Inc.

This will insure good draining. Set the post and hold or brace it while you plumb it with a level. Refer to Figs. 8-26 through 8-29.

Let's take a look at three popular fences: the board fence, the horizontal siding fence, and the contemporary screen fence. In Fig. 8-30 you can see

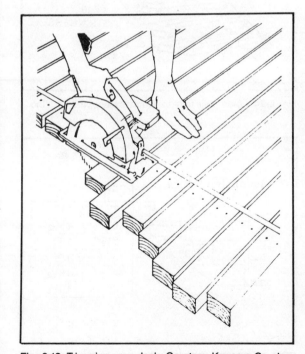

Fig. 8-18. Trimming your deck. Courtesy Koppers Co., Inc.

Fig. 8-20. Decorative deck railing. Courtesy Western Wood Products Assn.

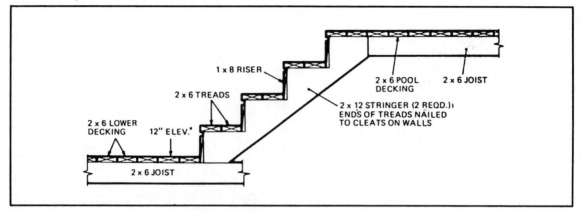

Fig. 8-21. Basic stair construction. Courtesy Western Wood Products Assn.

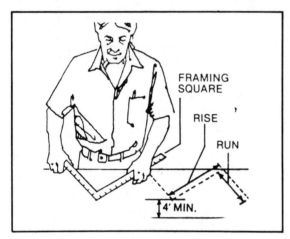

Fig. 8-22. Laying out the stair stringer. Courtesy Koppers Co., Inc.

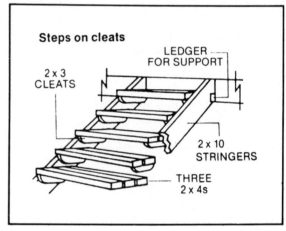

Fig. 8-24. Open stair design. Courtesy Koppers Co., Inc.

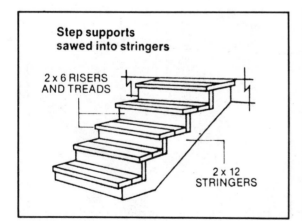

Fig. 8-23. Adding risers and treads. Courtesy Koppers Co., Inc.

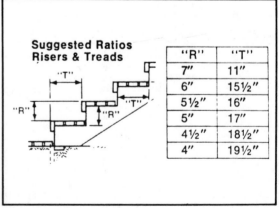

"R"	"T"
7"	11"
6"	15½"
5½"	16"
5"	17"
4½"	18½"
4"	19½"

Fig. 8-25. Table for building stair risers and treads. Courtesy Kelso.

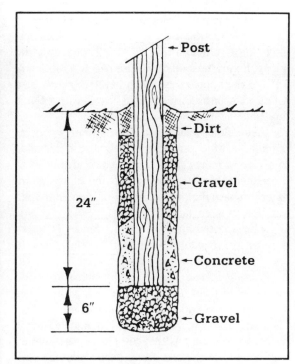

Fig. 8-26. Typical fence post hole. Courtesy Western Wood Products Assn.

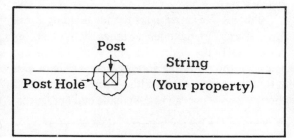

Fig. 8-27. Use string to outline your area to be fenced. Courtesy Western Wood Products Assn.

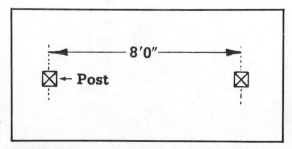

Fig. 8-28. Typical fence post spacing. Courtesy Western Wood Products Assn.

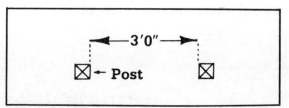

Fig. 8-29. Typical gate post spacing. Courtesy Western Wood Products Assn.

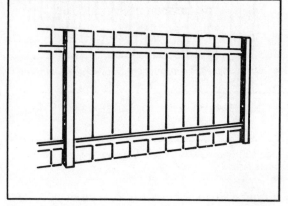

Fig. 8-30. Popular board fence. Courtesy Western Wood Products Assn.

Fig. 8-31. Alternating panel fence. Courtesy Western Wood Products Assn.

Fig. 8-32. Spaced board fence. Courtesy Western Wood Products Assn.

a typical side view of a board fence popular with swimming pool owners. The surface material can be any width of 1-inch boards, spaced 1 inch apart. The standard height is 5 feet, but this fence easily adapts to any height. The alternating panel fence offers a bolder pattern (Fig. 8-31). Boards of the same size or of random widths may be used. A spaced board design (Fig. 8-32), 6 inches apart, permits location near a house and eliminates the closed-in feeling.

The horizontal siding fence (Fig. 8-33) offers a number of practical uses. You can use a 3/4-inch beveled siding to match that on your house, creating a long, luxurious look. A top cap of 1 × 6 (optional) adds to the appearance. With beveled boards, use a 1-inch lap, or overlap standard boards with a 1-inch lap. Refer to Fig. 8-34.

A double-beveled fence is an extremely popular team project for you and your neighbor, if it is used to divide property. This fence is also attractive as a connector between the garage and house, as an exterior space divider, or as a visual screen to hide garbage cans or garden tools.

The contemporary screen fence is very popular with pool owners as it offers beauty and some privacy while allowing breezes through it. To build it, use 1 × 2s or rip pieces of 1 5/8 inches wide from larger boards. Set posts 4 feet apart. Preserve and stain 1-×-2-foot boards before installation as it will make your job much easier. 1 × 2s can be nailed as they are placed, then nailed occasionally to the 2-×-4-foot posts. Start by nailing 2 × 2s between the two post pieces. Next, begin stacking and nailing the alternating boards and spacers.

Table 8-5 offers a parts list for building these three fences. To make fences taller than 5 feet, order boards to the desired height. When increasing height of the posts, be sure to increase the depth in the ground for stability. It's also advisable to add another 2-×-4-foot rail in the middle of taller fences.

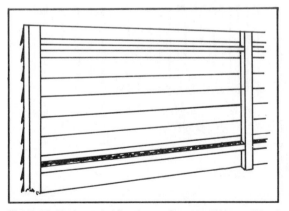

Fig. 8-33. Horizontal siding fence. Courtesy Western Wood Products Assn.

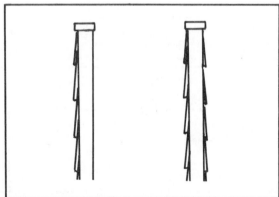

Fig. 8-34. Detail of horizontal siding fence. Courtesy Western Wood Products Assn.

Table 8-6. Parts List for Three Popular Pool Fences. Courtesy Western Wood Products Assn.

Board Fence Alternating Board or Panel	4 × 4 posts	2 × 4 rails	1 × 4	1 × 6	1 × 8	1 × 10	1 × 12
Number of pieces	2	2	21	16	11	9	8

Horizontal Siding Fence	4 × 4 posts	2 × 4 rails	Pieces 8′ long — using 1″ overlap				
			1 × 4	1 × 6	1 × 8	1 × 10	1 × 12
Number of pieces	2	2	22	13	9	7	6

| Contemporary Screen Fence | 2 × 4 posts | 2 × 4 post blocks | 1 × 2 blocks 9 | 1 × 2 blocks 15 | 1 × 2 boards 8′ 0″ | 2 × 2 rail 8′0″ | |
| Number of pieces | 4 | 2 | 17 | 18 | 36 | 1 | |

NOTE: To make fences taller than 5'0", order boards to desired length. When increasing height of posts, be sure to increase depth in ground for stability.
It is advisable to add another 2 × 4 rail in the middle of taller fences.

INSTALLING A CHAIN LINK FENCE

Many swimming pool owners prefer chain link fencing. This allows full view of the pool area, more air circulation, and improved security over many types of wood fences.

There are eight simple steps to installing a chain link fence around your swimming pool:

- ☐ Survey property lines.
- ☐ Locate and set terminal posts.
- ☐ Locate and set line posts.
- ☐ Apply fittings to terminal posts.
- ☐ Apply top rail.
- ☐ Hang fabric.
- ☐ Stretch fabric.
- ☐ Hang gates.

Tools you'll need include a posthole digger, fence stretcher, wire grip and stretch bar, cutting pliers, an adjustable end wrench, tape measure, and a carpenter's level.

Chain link "fabric" is made of wire and measured by gauge. The smaller the gauge number, the bigger—and stronger—the wire. The size of the wire mesh is also important. It is determined by measuring the distance between the parallel sides of the mesh. Common sizes are 2 1/8 inches and 2 inches. Larger mesh takes less steel to make and is not as costly.

Gates around your swimming pool should be of a sturdy construction with strong hinges, latches, and gateposts for long, trouble-free service. Make sure that the gate offers a large enough opening to accommodate anything you will need to take into the swimming pool area, such as lawn furniture. Also decide whether you want your gate to have an automatic latching device or a locking latch for added security.

Again, for a more detailed discussion of how to select and install a chain link fence, including industry standards, refer to *The Complete Book of Fences* (TAB Book No. 1508).

LANDSCAPING YOUR POOL

Just as with your home, landscaping can help beautify and improve your swimming pool area. With carefully planned landscaping you can give your pool site the look of a colonial garden, a tropical lagoon, a mountain lake, or a jungle paradise. If nothing else, you can lift an average pool to a decorative one.

There are also more practical reasons for

planting the grounds around your pool. Privacy is an important factor. Also, if cold winds are prevalent, a hedge or small trees can provide a sheltering effect. Plants and flowers will help reduce erosion around your newly installed pool.

But plantings close to the pool require careful selection and placement. Mistakes here can prove costly, either by actual damage to the pool and its filtering system, in the loss of expensive plants, or excessive cleaning and maintenance problems. The large tree that spreads its picturesque limbs over the pool may be beautiful, but it will certainly tax your filter system with excessive leaves and dirt.

Problem plants around pools include small-leafed deciduous plants and trees that can quickly wreck a pool filter by working it to death. Roses shouldn't be planted around a pool for the shedding of pedals and their attraction of insects. Hedges and border plants that require special maintenance should also be avoided. Plants that throw off fuzzy propagations that could clog the pool are also poor selections for areas near your pool.

If not these plants, then what? Landscape experts often recommend the use of permanent plants rather than annuals around a swimming pool. Ideal landscaping includes large-leafed plants like aralia pariferus, aralia saboldi, acanthas mollis, selloum philodendron, and melianthus major. If the climate permits, any palm tree or aralia papriferus can be allowed to overhang a pool where you want a tropical effect with a minimum of shedding.

TREES AND POOLS

Trees offer a special problem to pool owners, but not one without a solution. The roots of trees planted near a pool can crack the sides of the pool or interfere with underground piping and drains. One solution is to make the roots of trees grow downward instead of toward the pool wall. This is done by deep-watering the roots.

To deep-water a tree, sink three or four 3-foot long and 3-inch diameter plastic or clay pipes down into the soil locating them in a circle around the base of the tree. The bottom few inches of these pipes should be perforated with holes to let water seep through. Trees are watered periodically by running water into the pipes until the soil below is saturated.

LANDSCAPING SLOPES

Swimming pools often are installed in sloping or hillside locations. These placements require special consideration from a landscaping standpoint as well. Not only do they afford excellent opportunities for attractive landscaping, but if neglected, can cause considerable damage through erosion and landslide. For safety, anything more than a 9-foot rise should have an engineered concrete block retaining wall to support it. Smaller rises can often be braced with dry rock retaining walls that will add beauty as well as support to the hill.

Steep banks falling down to your swimming area should also be landscaped for beauty and practicality. You can often turn such a bank into a rustic rock garden by spotting colorful rocks along its slope and planting the spaces in between with small, deep-rooted bushes and creepers. The deep-rooted cover plants serve to bind the soil together and prevent it from washing away, possibly into your pool.

The rocks also provide good water shed by breaking up the force of cascading water. Rocks should be anchored into the soil by making sure that at least one third of their bulk is buried in the ground. This will both reduce the chance for movement and add a more natural look to the landscaping.

Flat pool areas can also be improved with landscaping. Mounds can be built to develop ground contour and to highlight specific plantings around the pool. Remember that mounds should have peat moss, mulch, and fertilizer added as they are built to insure that plants will grow.

Paths can also be laid around your pool to improve beauty and function. Such paths can be built of dimensional lumber, rough wood, rocks, cement steps, or numerous other materials that are designed to blend in with the landscaping and mood of your pool site.

LANDSCAPING IDEAS

There are as many ways of adding beauty and

function to your pool with landscaping as there are pools. Planters can be arranged around one end of the pool across from where sunbathers congregate. A trellis can be installed for both beauty and shade as long as it is planned so that leaves will not interfere with the pool's filtering system.

Waterfalls are a natural addition to many pools. Waterfalls can be built from stone or masonry or even plastic. In designing a pool waterfall, plan numerous shelves and pockets allowing the water to trickle down to be recycled or flow into the pool.

If the water is added to the pool, make sure that it is included within the filtering system. There should be no dirt or debris within the waterfall that could harm the filter.

The best way to design your pool landscaping is to study the ideas of others and improve upon them as you adapt to your own conditions. You can improve your pool's function and attractiveness by adding individualized enclosures, fences, decks, and landscaping.

Chapter 9

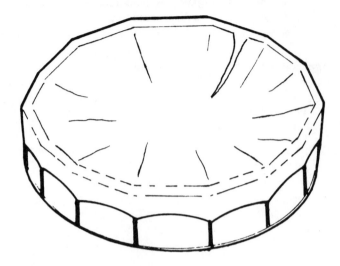

Pool Maintenance

The secret of having fun with your pool is keeping maintenance both easy and sufficient (Fig. 9-1). You don't want to spend more time keeping it up than enjoying it, yet you do want to insure that your pool is ready when you are. It's a balance that can be difficult to maintain without proper planning and application.

In this chapter you'll learn how to handle the daily and weekly chores that come with maintaining your pool's water system, the monthly and annual chores, and how to winterize your pool so it will be ready next spring. You'll also learn how to handle the repairs that come up in most pool systems.

Even if you already own and enjoy your pool, this chapter will offer useful information that can be worth the price of this book.

WATER TREATMENT

Regular care is the secret to full enjoyment of your family pool. It should be your desire to have a clean, disinfected pool at all times. The most com-

mon disinfectant used in swimming pools today is chlorine, as you learned in Chapter 5. This product is available in numerous familiar compounds. All of the chlorine products available on the market should prove to be satisfactory if they are used according to the manufacturer's recommendations.

In addition to the stated functions of killing bacteria and controlling algae, chlorine provides an additional important function: it reduces organic matter in the water. This is accomplished through the process of *oxidation* (a form of burning). The chlorine actually reduces organic material to a smaller form.

For chlorine to perform its function the residual, as registered on a test set, must be at least 0.3 to 0.6 parts per million *at all times*. If the newer stabilized chlorines are used, at least 1.0 parts per million is recommended. To prevent undissolved chlorine from settling on vinyl pool liners, remember to add the chlorine through the skimmer with the filter running.

Chlorine is only effective if it has an opportunity to kill bacteria, aid in algae control, and reduce

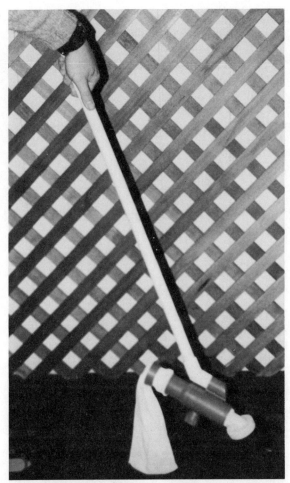
Fig. 9-1. Garden hose bag-type vacuum.

organic material. The success of chlorine is determined by both the proper chlorine residual in the pool and proper pH control. What is pH?

The measurement of alkalinity or acidity of the water contained in the swimming pool is called *pH*. It is measured on a scale from 1 to 14 with 7 as a theoretical neutral. For proper chlorine function, pH must be retained at a level between 7.2 and 7.6—slightly alkaline. This condition is maintained by using a reliable pool water test every day following manufacturer's procedures.

If the pH is below 7.2, the pool is considered over-acid. It must then be corrected by the addition of an alkaline material, such as sodium bicarbonate or soda ash, following the directions on the

manufacturer's container. If the pH is above 7.6, the pool water is overalkaline. It must be corrected by the addition of acid material, such as sodium bisulphate or muriatic acid.

Why is pH important to the function and comfort of your pool? If pH is approaching the acid side (below 7.2), skin and eye irritation will result. This low pH reading also causes the chlorine to become very unstable, and because of this, it is dissipated. Therefore, it doesn't have the time to perform its three basic functions: to kill algae, to kill bacteria, and to destroy organic matter.

If the pH is above 7.6, the water is overalkaline. This condition causes the chlorine to combine with other materials in the water such as ammonia. When chlorine is in a combined state, it is not available to perform its three basic functions. A pH above 7.6 also results in eye irritation to swimmers.

Let's take a look at the conditions which will exist when chlorine is in a combined state and, therefore, is not performing its necessary functions.

1. A strong odor of chlorine. This is not found when chlorine and pH are in balance.
2. A high test of chlorine on a test set; however, this is a reading of chlorine in a nonfunctional form.
3. The pool water tends to be grayish or cloudy.
4. Swimmers complain of eye irritation. This is not a normal reaction of bathers to chlorine when chlorine is in its proper state.

POOL CHEMICAL BALANCE

To correct the conditions of combined chlorine and almost all normal water problems, you should follow this procedure:

1. Adjust the pH to the range of 7.2 to 7.6. This pH will allow the chlorine to be available to kill bacteria, to kill and control algae, and to destroy organic matter.
2. *Super-chlorinate* or "shock the pool." Both of these terms mean to add three to five times the normal dosage of chlorine to the pool. With an adjusted pH, this super-

125

chlorinization will drive off the unstable forms of chlorine which cannot be restored to a usable state. It will replace them with chlorine in its proper pH environment and will be ready to do its job.

3. It's a good practice to super-chlorinate once every two or three weeks.
4. It's best to add acid material in the morning. Chlorine should be added in the early evening.

POOL CARE TIPS

In addition to cleaning and disinfecting the water through the use of purification agents, the water should also be kept free of foreign material. One way to do this is to use flagstone, brick, or concrete around the pool area to prevent excessive amounts of grass and dirt from being carried into the pool on swimmer's feet.

Another method is to use a filter and skimmer. The best filter systems include a surface skimmer which traps bugs, leaves, grass, etc. The "strained" water is then forced through the main filtering unit and reenters the pool sparkling clean.

A third way to keep your pool free of foreign material is to remove sediment from the pool bottom. You can use a pool vacuum used with a pool filter or a bag-type vacuum used with garden hose pressure (Fig. 9-1).

Fiberglass and vinyl liners are especially sensitive to damage if abused. To insure long pool life, don't use metallic items in and around your pool. Swimmers should not wear shoes of any kind. In fact, swim fins are discouraged since many are semirigid and contain metal buckles which may damage the liner or finish. Be sure to keep sticks and other sharp objects away from the pool. Avoid using hard toys in the pool. Keep the family pet out of the pool. Finally, don't jump or dive into your pool unless it is designed for safe diving.

POOL MAINTENANCE CHECKLIST

To make the maintenance of your pool's system more efficient, here is a simple pool maintenance checklist used by many pool owners:

1. Skim pool surface.
2. Brush walls and floor (Fig. 9-2).
3. Scrub tile.
4. Clean out skimmer.
5. Vacuum pool.
6. Clean out leaf strainer.

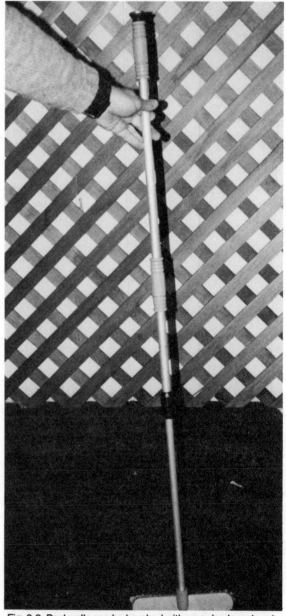

Fig. 9-2. Pool walls can be brushed with a garden hose brush.

7. Check filter pressure.

8. Hose down deck.

Simple enough. Remember to check the pump, filter, and circulation system periodically. Clean the filter often for optimum water clarity.

WINTERIZING YOUR POOL

Too soon your swimming season is over and it's time to prepare your pool for hibernation until spring. How extensive this is depends upon the type of pool you own and the kind of weather offered in a typical winter. To simplify, here are the steps required to winterize the "typical" pool.

First, vacuum your swimming pool out. Adjust the pH, allowing it to stabilize before closing the pool up.

Second, add winterizing chemicals as recommended by your pool dealer. Let the filter run to circulate the chemicals. If you are using a winter tab dispenser, be sure to tie it securely so it cannot sink and stain a vinyl pool. Your dealer can make specific recommendations based on local weather and water conditions.

Third, lower the water level in your swimming pool to approximately 1 inch below the skimmer.

Next, disconnect the filter and the pump from the circulation lines. Drain all lines thoroughly making especially sure that water is not trapped in them. It could freeze during the winter causing extensive damage to equipment.

Remember to place winter plugs in all inlets and outlets. If winter plugs didn't come with your pool, you can often purchase them where you buy pool chemicals.

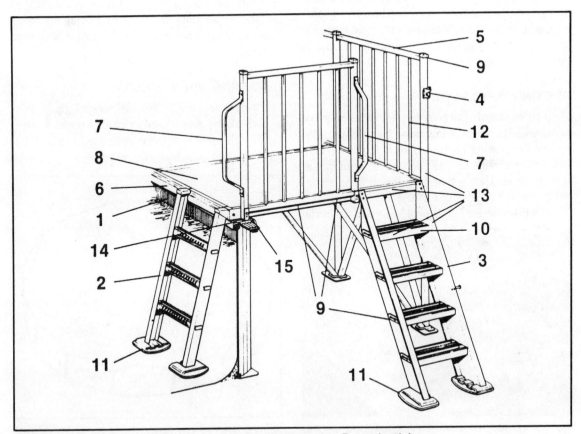

Fig. 9-3. Remove ladders and other equipment. Courtesy Doughboy Recreational, Inc.

Fig. 9-4. Cover your swimming pool for the winter.

Sixth, remove all diving boards, ladders, and other equipment from the pool (Fig. 9-3). Store them in your garage or other building where they will not be subjected to the harshness of winter.

Finally, cover your swimming pool with a solid cover (Figs. 9-4 and 9-5) or anchored cover available from your pool dealer. Make sure that you drain excess water from the top of the cover from time to time during the winter months.

OPENING YOUR POOL

The wind tears calendar pages from their place as autumn leaves, blowing snow, and pelting rain signify the passing of the seasons. Finally, spring has arrived and it's time to open up the pool for another season. Here's how to prepare your swimming pool for a new year of use.

If you winterized your pool last year, drain the

Fig. 9-5. Your pool cover can be easily rolled and unrolled using this cover storage mechanism.

water off the cover and remove it.

Remove any plugs and ice protection devices. Store them for next winter.

Check the liner or walls over carefully. Clean any built-up dirt from the pool walls.

Raise the pool's water level back to the proper height. Then vacuum any debris in the pool and backwash the filter to clear out the debris and built-up scum.

Check and add conditioner. Super-chlorinate as outlined earlier or according to manufacturer's instructions. Balance the pool water's pH and total alkalinity.

Finally, establish your free chlorine residual and regular maintenance program. Once down to safe swimming levels, you're ready to enjoy the pool once again.

Keeping the pool physically clean is not really that difficult once a regular routine is established and the proper equipment is used. During the swimming season, thoroughly clean the pool at least once a week.

REPAIRING VINYL LINERS

Vinyl liners are becoming increasingly popular in both above-ground and in-ground pools. However, they do require special attention to insure that they do their job: hold the water.

Fig. 9-6. Tears in vinyl liners should be quickly repaired. Courtesy Doughboy Recreational, Inc.

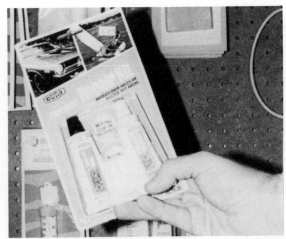

Fig. 9-7. Vinyl liner repair kits are available through most pool supply firms.

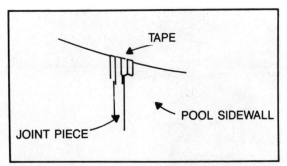

Fig. 9-9. Repairing a metal wall pool joint. Courtesy Heldor Associates, Inc.

Small tears and punctures (Fig. 9-6) in the liner may be repaired quickly with a repair patch kit (Fig. 9-7) available with your pool or through the dealer. Directions for use are included. Repair is a simple process, depending on location and size.

For major repairs to the vinyl liner, metal wall, or frame, contact your dealer or write the manufacturer directly. There may be a simple solution to your problem, or it may be one that only the manufacturer can remedy. In any case, don't attempt to make major repairs before talking with a professional.

Manufacturers recommend that you lower the water level every two years to a point where you can pull the liner away from the sidewall and inspect the inside of the wall for rust spots (Fig. 9-8). This should be less than a 1-foot drop in water level. If rust is found, remove the rust with steel wool and apply a rust-preventative material. If it looks like the rust is prevalent below the 1-foot depth, you will have to remove the water and liner completely (Figs. 9-9 through 9-11).

With the liner removed, reinstall the seats and proceed to sand any rusted areas and paint with Rust-o-leum or equivalent. This may require removing the earth cove. If you have done this, replace the cove after the paint has thoroughly dried (Fig. 9-12). At this time, check your liner to be sure that it has not deteriorated in any areas. If it appears that you need a new liner, reinstall as outlined in Chapter 4.

Remember, if you have any questions about your pool frame, liner, or siding (Fig. 9-13), contact your pool dealer. Most have the experience to make

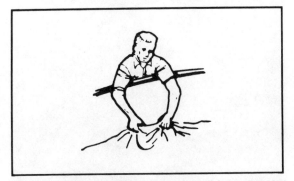

Fig. 9-8. Inspect the inside of the sidewall for rust spots. Courtesy Doughboy Recreational, Inc.

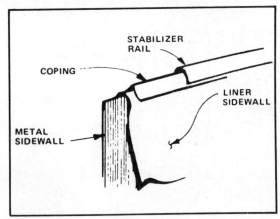

Fig. 9-10. Reinstalling the vinyl pool liner. Courtesy Doughboy Recreational, Inc.

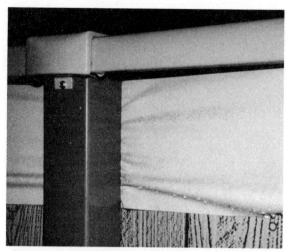

Fig. 9-11. Moisture on the outside of the pool wall can indicate a problem.

pool maintenance and repair simpler. In many cases they can make recommendations that will eliminate the problem and increase pool enjoyment.

PAINTING YOUR POOL

Swimming pools provide the means for inexpensive, healthful recreation and for one of the best forms of human exercise. They can be constructed almost anywhere and don't require expensive individual equipment. A swimming pool is most attractive and the greatest benefits result from its use when the water is sparkling; the walls, bottoms,

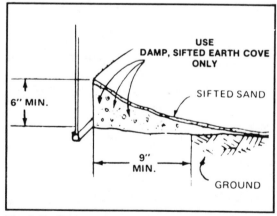

Fig. 9-12. Replace the earth cove. Courtesy Doughboy Recreational, Inc.

sides, and surrounding areas are clean; and proper surfaces are painted in contrasting but compatible colors.

It is very important from a safety factor that pools be painted. The visibility at the deep end of unpainted pools is very poor. When the pool is crowded, someone could be on the bottom of the pool drowning and be unseen and unnoticed. Unpainted pools cannot be properly cleaned, creating a breeding place for algae.

Paint also helps protect the pool and its accessories from exposure to weather and water. Proper painting will greatly retard the slow disintegration of concrete and delay expensive repair jobs. Any paint selected should be specifically a swimming pool paint.

SURFACE PREPARATION

Fresh concrete undergoes considerable changes

Fig. 9-13. Repaired pool frame and liner.

as it dries. At first it contains a great deal of water, and painting should be deferred for at least ten days—or longer under poor drying conditions. Of this time at least three days should be hot and dry to allow the concrete to cure properly.

Concrete Pools

Special surface preparation is necessary because of the severe conditions of exposure naturally present around a pool. Paint which doesn't have a secure bond to a properly prepared surface doesn't perform satisfactorily.

Any concrete must be thoroughly cleaned before painting. All new concrete should be etched to clean the concrete and give a good base to which the paint can adhere. Since concrete is etched with acid, the person using the acid must be protected with rubber boots, rubber gloves, and goggles. A 10 percent solution of muriatic acid gives satisfactory results. This acid is readily available at hardware or farm supply stores. Since it is usually sold in stronger concentrations, it should be properly diluted with water to reduce it to 10 percent. Carefully follow the handling instructions on the label.

The prepared acid is poured onto the concrete and distributed with long-handled, stiff bristle brushes. The acid must be kept in contact with the surface until the effervescense or bubbling stops. The entire surface must then be *thoroughly rinsed* and, at the same time, brushed to dislodge loose material. It is very important to remove *all* acid used in etching. New concrete patches on old pools should also be etched before painting.

If any cracks are noted in the new pool, they must be filled. Be sure the concrete is dry and the crack is free of loose dust. Use a sealant which is recommended for concrete swimming pools and follow the manufacturer's directions to the letter. If a primer is recommended in the cracks before sealing, use the type recommended for the sealant to be used. Force the sealant into the crack as far as possible. Smooth the sealant flush with the surrounding concrete surface. *Do not* use a black mastic filler (asphalt type) for this purpose.

The preparation of a previously painted concrete pool depends upon the condition of the paint. If the old paint is in good condition, a good scrubbing with a nonsoap detergent will prepare it for a new coat of paint. If mildew or fungus is present (usually appearing as dark areas) it must be killed and removed by using a cleaner containing sodium hypochlorite or one containing trisodium phosphate. Scrub until all traces of mildew are removed and rinse thoroughly.

If the old paint is cracked, peeling, or has a very powdery surface which won't wash off, it may be best to remove all paint down to the concrete surface. The most complete method is sandblasting. Small pools may sometimes be cleaned of old paint by using a power sander. After the paint is removed, use an acid wash to clean the pores of the concrete from the sanding operation. Follow a procedure like the acid etch operation, except the acid solution in this case may be weaker than that used on new concrete. Follow with a trisodium phosphate wash to neutralize the acid, then rinse thoroughly with water. All cracks should be patched with concrete before the acid wash so the patches may be etched by the acid. Cracks should be filled with sealant as in the case of a new pool.

Metal Pools

New steel pools should be sandblasted before priming. A rust-inhibiting primer should be applied immediately after sandblasting to prevent rusting prior to painting. Your contractor should do this during the installation of the pool. Remember that any accumulation of rust must be removed before you begin to paint. For rust spots and small patches of rust, a chemical rust remover, such as Naval Jelly, may be used.

Metal pools constructed of material other than steel are not generally sandblasted. They must be cleaned with a solvent to remove oil and grease, then washed with a nonsoap detergent and rinsed before painting. The primer should be applied as soon as the pool is dry to prevent dirt collection and the beginning of corrosion.

In the case of metal pools which have been previously painted, and if the paint is not cracked, peeled or excessively powdery, a good scrubbing with a nonsoap detergent is recommended. When thoroughly rinsed and dry, the pool may be given a fresh coat of paint. If the paint is in poor condition and corrosion is present, the old paint should be removed. Sandblasting is generally the best procedure in this case, then proceed as with a new pool.

TYPES OF PAINT

Paints which are applied to concrete must be resistant to alkali since there is an excess of alkali present in concrete at all times. Some paint vehicles react with alkali, and when this happens, the paint film is ruined. Such paints must be avoided when painting concrete.

Concrete Pools

The most widely used paint for concrete pools are:

- □ *Rubber-based, solvent-thinned type.* These are one-package enamels offered by many manufacturers in a variety of suitable colors.
- □ *Catalyzed epoxy, solvent-thinned type.* These are two-package enamels offered in a variety of colors for pools. The two components are mixed before use and generally have a pot life of at least eight hours after mixing.

Both types, if used according to the manufacturer's directions and applied carefully, will give excellent service on concrete pools. These paints contain strong solvents and must be used over old paints with caution as "lifting" of the old paint may occur. It is a good idea to try a small patch of coating over old paint to determine if wrinkling of the previous coat occurs.

Metal Pools

A good general rule in selecting paint for a new metal pool is to be sure the primer and topcoat paints are components of the same system. One way to assure this is to buy the two coatings from the same manufacturer and follow his recommendations. Rubber-based paints, catalyzed epoxy

coatings, and solution vinyl systems have all been used successfully on metal pools if the primer is an epoxy type, it is usually best to use an epoxy topcoat. The same is true of vinyl systems. In buying coatings for metal pools, identify the type of metal to your reputable paint dealer and follow his guidance for the specific paint system to use. It is important to follow label directions concerning drying time between coats. This may be the difference in getting a good or poor paint job.

Color is an important factor to consider before painting a pool. A well-painted pool is inviting and gives the impression that it is sanitary and well maintained. The ironwork around the pool—ladders, fences, life guard seats, etc.—presents an opportunity to improve the appearance of the pool. After the anticorrosive primer has been applied, apply one of the many colors of exterior enamel available. Aluminum paint also gives a pleasing effect.

APPLICATION

The method of application of the paint is subject to personal preference, equipment available, and the surface of the concrete. Brushes, spray guns, or rollers can be used to coat pools. Directions on the can will suggest the best ways to apply a particular coating. Whatever the method used, it is necessary to insure that all pits and crevices are painted.

No painting should be started when the surface is damp or wet. The temperature should be warm—above 50° F.—to assure the formation of strong paint films. Label directions may specify temperature ranges in which special coatings can be applied. Painting should be done in the shade if possible. Paint sets too rapidly in hot sunshine, and lap marks or blisters may result. You may want to set up a temporary sun screen with plywood sheets while painting on a warm day.

The label instructions should be followed as to the drying time necessary between coats. Remember to allow plenty of drying time after painting before filling the pool with water. Filling the pool too quickly after painting has been responsible for many paint failures. A week or longer of warm drying weather is a good general rule to follow.

Fig. 9-14. Periodically inspect the footing and base of your above-ground pool for signs of leakage or damage.

POOL PAINTING HINTS

A painted pool that is in good condition except for a few spots can be touched up to avoid a complete repainting. It is important to remove all loose paint and smooth the edges of the bare spots. This can be done with sandpaper or a wire brush.

If any influence can be exerted when the pool is built, a little foresight then will prevent disfigurement of the paint later. A concrete pool should have a waterproof coating on the outside before the backfill is placed. Water which penetrates the walls or bottom from the outside can cause blisters even with alkali-resistant paints. It is also important to coat the back side of metal pools when they are constructed to prevent corrosion.

ESTIMATING PAINT REQUIREMENTS

It's most economical to accurately estimate the amount of paint you need to refinish your swimming pool. By making a good estimate you can reduce waste and use the money you save to purchase between paint.

Here's a quick way to figure the number of square feet of surface in your pool so you can calculate the amount of paint you need. The example is based on a pool 20 feet wide by 40 feet long by 6 feet deep. We want to come up with a total floor area and a total wall area:

Floor area:
20' × 40' =   800 sq. ft.

Wall area:
2 end walls @ 20' ea.	=	40'
2 side walls @ 40' ea.	=	80'
Total wall distance around	=	120'
Multiply by wall height × 6'	=	720 sq. ft.

Total surface   1520 sq. ft.
area to be painted

In this example, you will need enough swimming pool paint to cover approximately 1520 square feet. To be safe, add 10 to 20 percent for a coverage of 1672 to 1824 square feet. Then, check with numerous paint dealers about the correct type of paint for your pool, using the coverage figure estimated. A paint that covers 1750 square feet would be ideal and probably give you a small amount left over for touch-up.

What if your pool is of varied depth? Then break up the wall into easy-to-measure sections and

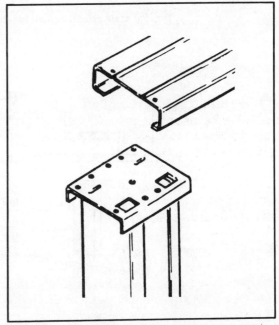

Fig. 9-15. The pool seats should be regularly inspected for rust. Courtesy Doughboy Recreational, Inc.

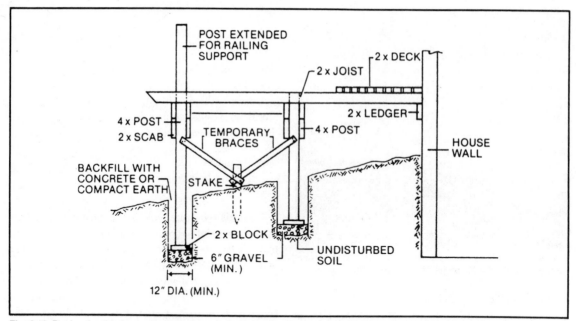

Fig. 9-16. Decks should also be inspected regularly. Temporary braces should be installed until repair is completed. Courtesy Koppers Co., Inc.

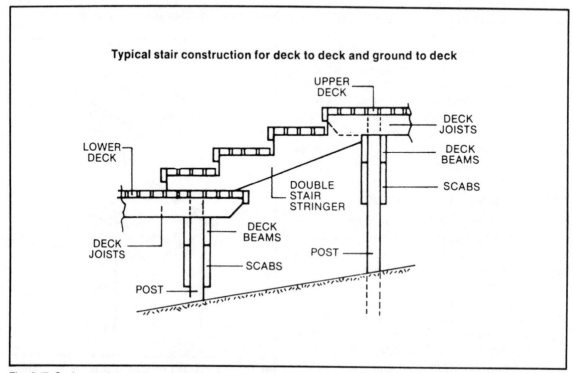

Typical stair construction for deck to deck and ground to deck

Fig. 9-17. Scabs can be used as temporary repairs to decks and stairs. Courtesy Koppers Co., Inc.

add them up. Average them for the wall height figure above.

Remember, too, that manufacturer's coverage estimates are just that: estimates. They can vary widely depending upon a number of conditions, including the weather, the type and condition of concrete in your pool, and the method of application. Sometimes it's more efficient to purchase a larger amount of paint than return later for a small can.

MAINTAINING YOUR POOL

As with any major purchase, it is usually less expensive to develop an efficient maintenance schedule for your pool and stick to it than to make emergency repairs as required. Also, such emergencies usually occur when the pool is most heavily used, such as during the summer months and on holiday weekends.

Hopefully, this chapter has given you some good ideas for making your own maintenance list for daily, weekly, monthly, and annual checkups of your pool's condition and catching problems before they occur (Figs. 9-14 through 9-17). Once you've developed your list, be sure to post it in a prominent location, such as your pool chemical storage area or pump house, to remind you of the needed steps. The list will also be helpful for family members, housesitters, and pool maintenance people called in. Keep filter, heater, and other equipment booklets here, too.

Chapter 10

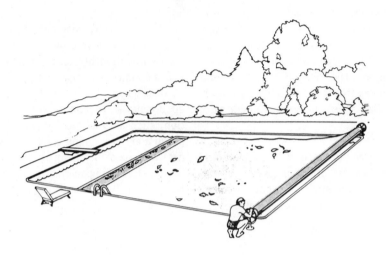

Pool Safety

Is swimming safe? The U.S. Consumer Product Safety Commission estimates there are over 434,000 accidents associated with playing basketball each year, while 126,000 accidents occur in and around swimming pools. Most of these involve cuts, scrapes, and bruises. Yet more than twice as many people participate in swimming each year than in basketball.

Swimming is safe—provided that pools are designed for safety and swimmers understand the concepts of safe swimming (Fig. 10-1). When properly installed and equipped, a swimming pool can be a source of fun for the whole family (Fig. 10-2). Although swimming pools were formerly considered a safety hazard, recent facts and figures have shown that such a belief is incorrect.

For example, it was once though that diving is the primary cause of spinal injuries. Actually, about 50 percent of the reported spinal cord injuries are caused by automobile accidents, 20 percent by falls, and only 12 percent from diving. Of the estimated 500 serious spinal cord injuries each year that occur from diving, three out of four occur in lakes,

rivers, and natural aquatic environments rather than in man-made swimming pools. Another fact: nine out of ten diving accidents that occur in swimming pools happen in the shallow water and not in areas designed for diving (Fig. 10-3).

Of the 7,000 total drownings that occur each year, 450 are related to residential and public swimming pools, according to National Safety Council statistics. The number of pools in use has increased 400-fold between 1948 and 1980, while the number of drownings has *decreased* by one-third.

Why are swimming pools safer and injuries less likely? Many reasons. One is because the government and manufacturers have regulated or voluntarily improved swimming pools for safety. Another is the work of the American National Red Cross in teaching safe aquatics. Most important is the consumer awareness that has developed over the past few decades that is expressed in buyers' concern over pool safety.

PLANNING POOL SAFETY

There are many safety factors to consider as you

Fig. 10-1. Pools offer safe fun for family and friends. Courtesy NSPI.

can go before the water is over their heads. The slope can be more acute where depths are 5 1/2 feet or more, such as in the diving end.

If you're planning a diving board, make sure there will be at least 7 1/2 feet of water to dive into. There should be at least 6 feet of deep water on either side of the board and 8 feet in front of it. This clearance is necessary so that someone diving or falling from the diving board will not land in shallow water.

The walk around the pool and the coping at the edge should be made of materials which the bare foot can grip firmly. Tile with a semi-rough surface or concrete with tiny ridges will help insure that no one around the pool will slip and fall (Fig. 10-4).

You can also use decorative rope to mark off the shallow and deep sections of the pool. These lines serve to keep young bathers out of the deep end where they might be struck by a diver. The lines also give a swimmer something to hold onto if he has trouble in the water. These lines can make it

plan and build your swimming pool. To protect young children, the shallow end of the pool should slope no more than about one foot for every seven feet of length up to a depth of 5 1/2 feet. With this gentle slope, children won't misjudge how far they

Fig. 10-2. Above-ground pools minimize the hazard of children and pets inadvertently falling in. Courtesy Western Wood Products Assn.

Fig. 10-3. Most pool diving accidents occur in pools that are not designed for diving. Courtesy NSPI.

Fig. 10-4. The pool walkway should be of a semirough material. Courtesy NSPI.

138

difficult for a swim along the entire length of the pool, but, they can be placed and removed easily. You can use them when small children are in the pool and take them off when swimmers are doing laps.

SAFE POOL COVERS

Pool covers can be both efficient and safe to use (Figs. 10-5 through 10-10). Most covers will support a considerable amount of weight and offer additional protection in case someone accidentally falls into the pool. In addition, alarm systems can be installed to sound when an object or person enters the pool or the pool area.

In selecting a safe pool cover, consider one that is rigid enough and anchored well enough to support the weight of someone who might fall into the pool. Some pool covers will be floating types, others will be anchored to the swimming deck. Other types will have special tracks that allow them to roll out from storage to cover the pool.

As mentioned earlier though, make sure that a swimmer cannot inadvertently swim under the cover and become trapped. They may not be able to find a way out in time.

SAFETY EQUIPMENT

You should have life preservers near your swimming pool in case of emergency. A preserver can be hung on a nearby fence (Fig. 10-11) to be a decorative nautical element as well as a practical piece of equipment. The preserver should be attached to rope as long as the pool is wide so that it will reach a swimmer anywhere in the water.

Another useful pool safety tool is a pole with a shepherd's crook. It can be used to quickly give a swimmer something to grasp. The pole should be at least 12 feet long. Many people simply put a shepherd's hook on the other end of a standard pool net pole used for skimming debris in the water. Remember to keep it nearby so its is easy to grasp and use.

Fig. 10-5. Roll-up pool covers can offer both pool efficiency and safety. Courtesy Richardson Industries, Inc.

Fig. 10-6. Pool covers can be anchored to the deck. Courtesy Anchor Industries, Inc.

If you plan on having many young swimmers, consider a few life jackets that fit snugly around the chest. The old style loose water-rings are not safe as they can slip down the child's torso and actually hold him head down in the water.

SAFE LIGHTING

Lighting is an important safety element in your swimming pool system (Figs. 10-12 and 10-13). You should plan your pool area so that it can be completely lit for evening swimming or entertainment.

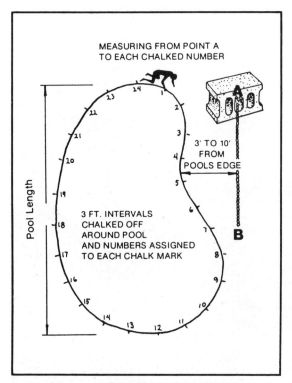

Fig. 10-7. Planning the installation of an anchored pool cover. Courtesy Anchor Industries, Inc.

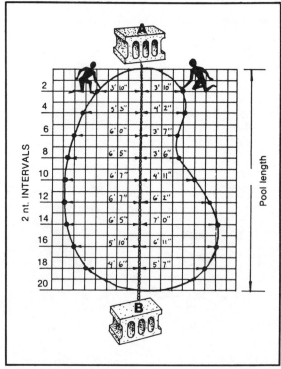

Fig. 10-8. Odd-shaped pools are more difficult to cover. Courtesy Anchor Industries, Inc.

Fig. 10-9. Pool cover for above-ground pool. Courtesy Richardson Industries, Inc.

You should also be able to quickly turn on the lights from inside the house and somewhere near the pool in case you hear a splash when the pool is not supposed to be in use.

Refer to *Effective Lighting For Home and Business* by Dan Ramsey (TAB Book No. 1658) for instructions on how to design and install your own outdoor lighting system.

POOL SAFETY RULES

Once you've insured that your pool is safe for use by young and old, the next step is to instruct swimmers on swim safety procedures. There are numerous useful charts (Fig. 10-14) that can be posted near the pool. Be sure the swimmers,

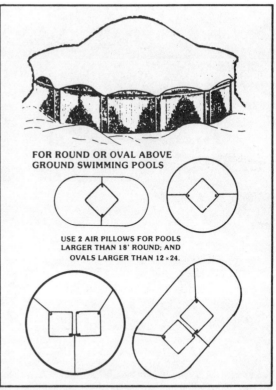

FOR ROUND OR OVAL ABOVE GROUND SWIMMING POOLS

USE 2 AIR PILLOWS FOR POOLS LARGER THAN 18' ROUND; AND OVALS LARGER THAN 12 × 24.

Fig. 10-10. Air pillow pool covers can be used in many sizes and shapes of pools. Courtesy Heldor Associates, Inc.

Fig. 10-11. Life preservers can be attached to a nearby fence. Courtesy NSPI.

Fig. 10-12. Pool lighting can be mounted and controlled from your home. Courtesy NSPI.

Fig. 10-13. Lanterns can be installed around the perimeter of your pool for festive evening entertainment. Courtesy NSPI.

Fig. 10-14. Pool safety signs are available through pool supply houses. Courtesy Doughboy Recreational, Inc.

especially children, know and obey these rules.

Here is a typical set of swimming pool safety rules that can be used for your pool:

No one may swim in the pool without specific permission from an adult. This regulation will stop youngsters from inviting friends in for a dip without parents' permission. It will make it necessary for every swimmer to be checked into the pool. A fenced pool will make it easier to enforce this rule.

No child may use the pool alone. Even good swimmers should have a "buddy"—someone to help them in case of sudden trouble, or at least to call for assistance.

Running around the pool, pushing others into the water, or any other kind of rough-housing is strictly forbidden. Regardless of his age, the show-off detracts from the pleasure of others. He is often a menace to safety because the danger of slipping, falling, and cracking one's head against the side of the pool is great when such horseplay is going on.

No one is to play with stones, hard balls, sticks, or other hard objects in or around the pool. A person struck by an object of this kind while in the water may lose consciousness. Remove any such objects from the pool area.

Playing games in the pool is forbidden unless a *good adult swimmer is on hand.* In a small home pool, games like tag or water polo should not be played by some swimmers while others try to enjoy normal swimming. When such games are played, those not taking part in them should leave the water. Preferably one adult should not take part in the game, but stand by to make sure that no player is hurt or endangered.

Only one person can stand on the diving board at a time. This rule will prevent youngsters from pushing anyone off or falling off while somebody else dives.

Repeated bouncing on the board and long or running dives are forbidden. The typical home pool is not large enough for such practices. A person who takes a long, running dive may land 10 or 15 feet away from the diving board, perhaps where the water is no more than 4 feet deep. A broken neck can result.

Dives can be made only from the board, not from the sides, of the pool. This rule is intended to make sure that only one person dives into the water at any given time. Divers should leave the diving area as soon as possible. Swimming in the deep end of the pool should be restricted while the diving board is in use.

Nonswimmers must remain out of the deep-water area. Parents should define the exact point to which their children can go. If your adult guests don't swim, tell them before they enter the pool how deep the water is at different points.

Allow at least one hour after eating before entering the water. A person who tries to swim just after a meal risks painful cramps. Schedule your pool usage for those times before meals or after a waiting period has elapsed.

Here are a few more smart swimming pool rules:

Be prepared for emergencies. You'll be able to relax and enjoy yourself more if you are prepared for emergencies. Basic lifesaving equipment should be provided at all times, and adults and older children should know how to use them.

Keep inebriated guests out of the pool. One study showed evidence of alcohol in the blood of 47 percent of adults who drowned. Pools and alcohol don't mix.

Keep breathing tubes near the pool. These simple, inexpensive plastic tubes can be fitted into the mouth of a swimmer pulled from the pool and used to give artificial respiration easily and safely.

PREVENTING DIVING ACCIDENTS

Since diving accidents can be among the most serious, let's take special consideration of safe diving procedures. Diving accidents, which cause some 500 spinal cord injuries a year in lakes, streams, and pools, can be prevented by knowing how to dive properly. Here are some tips to follow (Fig. 10-15):

- ☐ If you dive down, you must steer up immediately with your head and hands up.
- ☐ Keep your hands tipped up, your head back, and your back arched when diving. Don't dive too deep.
- ☐ Always keep your hands in front of your head.
- ☐ You must plan your dive path into the water before you dive.
- ☐ Don't dive into unknown waters. Make sure there are no submerged or floating obstacles.

- ☐ No back dives or running dives.
- ☐ Don't dive across the narrow part of a pool.
- ☐ Don't add diving equipment to pools not designed for diving.

According to research by the National Spa and Pool Institute, the overwhelming majority of swimming pool diving injuries occur in the shallow water. Their victims are largely males between the ages of 13 and 23. While the study looked carefully at pool design and diving boards as possible factors in diving accidents in man-made pools, it determined that requiring deeper pools would do little to solve the problem. The study showed that even if all of the nation's 4.24 million pools could magically be made 22 feet deep in the diving end, only about 5 percent of the serious diving injuries would be avoided.

The study estimated that 95 percent of the diving-related injuries occur in six feet of water or less. Three of four such injuries occur in less than four feet of water. So the solution to diving injuries is, in most cases, to make sure that diving is done in diving areas only.

One major problem is overcoming the urge to dive into above-ground pools. The majority are only 3 1/2 feet deep and most are not made for diving. One solution is to build the deck around the above-ground pool at ground level so that swimmers are not tempted to stand on the deck and dive off. You can also build a deck at rim height, but build a railing around the above-ground pool so that the water can only be entered through certain openings around ladders.

Swimming pool slides should not be installed except in pools that are designed for them. They should be of the correct depth and structure so that people using the slide will not be in water too deep or shallow for safety. Slides must not interfere with normal swimming activities and games being enjoyed by other swimmers.

SWIMMING POOL FUN

Safety considerations are important in planning and using your swimming pool. Also important is having fun (Fig. 10-16). Here are a number

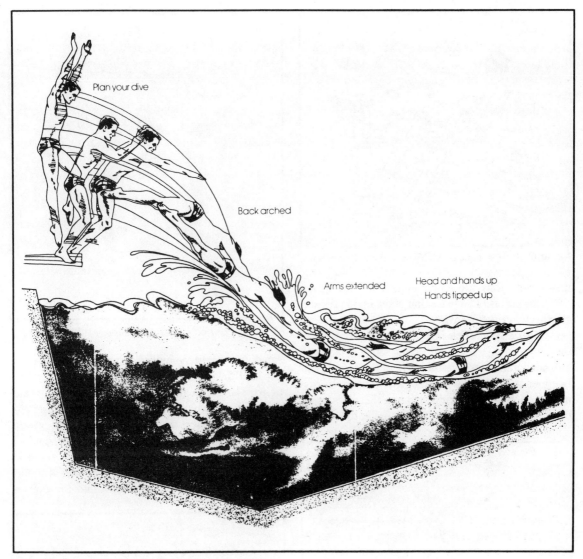

Fig. 10-15. Guidelines for safe diving. Courtesy NSPI.

of games that can be set up and played with little or no equipment, yet offer enjoyment and exercise (Figs. 10-17 to 10-23) for both children and adults.

Find the Match. One player is chosen to hide a wooden match stick. The other players meanwhile stand on the edge of the pool while he dives in and swims around and back to the side of the pool. He lets go of the match somewhere on the trip out or back. By the time he has reached the side of the pool, the match will have floated to the top. As soon

as any one of the players on the deck sees the match, he dives in to retrieve it. The player who gets the match then hides it in the next round.

Underwater Tag. Using the same rules as any form of land tag, the person who is "it" must tag another person while under the surface of the water.

Water Dodge Ball. This is a fun game for two large groups of players. One group forms a circle around the other and throws the ball at those

Fig. 10-16. Pools were made for fun. Courtesy Kuddle Kove.

inside until they are eliminated. Then the group switches places. The team that stays inside the circle the longest time wins.

High Diver. This is a jumping or diving contest that can increase your diving skills. Place two tall, anchored poles on either side of the pool directly opposite the highest point of a dive from the diving board. Stretch a string between the poles using clothes pins. The object of this game is to see who

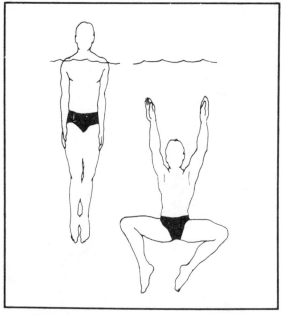

Fig. 10-18. Easy pool exercise. Courtesy NSPI.

can dive or jump the highest. Each time a successful trip over the string is made, it is raised slightly. Participants must be skilled divers, and the diving safety precautions mentioned earlier must be observed.

Poison. Here's a game for a small group. Everyone joins hands in a circle in the pool. A floating ball is placed in the center to serve as "poison." As soon as the starting whistle is sounded, everyone tries to pull others into the poison.

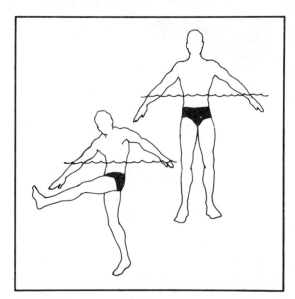

Fig. 10-17. Pools are an excellent place for exercise. Courtesy NSPI.

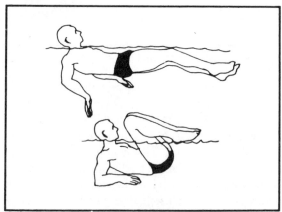

Fig. 10-19. Floating exercise. Courtesy NSPI.

146

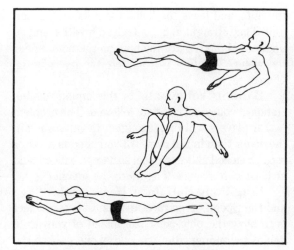

Fig. 10-20. Turning exercise. Courtesy NSPI.

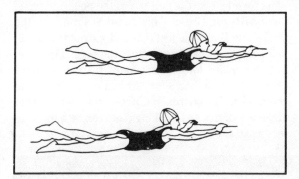

Fig. 10-21. Kicking exercise. Courtesy NSPI.

Fig. 10-22. Leg development exercises. Courtesy NSPI.

Anyone touching the poison must drop out and hands are rejoined. No ducking is allowed. Also, anyone who lets go in order to prevent being poisoned must drop out.

Still Waters. All players line up on one side of the pool. The referee stands outside the pool and calls "moving waters." Players start for the other side of the pool. When the referee calls "still waters," all swimmers stop moving and stay as motionless as they can. Any player caught moving must return to the starting line. The first player to reach the other side is the winner and may become the referee for the next game.

Pan Race. Remember the "Egg and the Spoon Race?" Here's the aquatic version. Players form a line along one side of the pool. Each player has a cake pan or similar vessel that will float when placed on the water. The object of the game is to push the pan with the chin to the other side of the pool. The first one there wins.

Ball Tag. Here's another good "tag" game. The one who is "it" tries to hit another player with an inflated rubber or plastic ball. The player who is tagged becomes "it." This game can be played in either the deep or shallow end of the pool.

May I? In this game, all players line up on one side of the pool. The one who is "it" stands in the water at the other side. Each player is called by name and is told in which manner he or she may move forward, such as: "John, you may backstroke four strokes forward." Each player must say "May I?" before moving. "It" then says, "Yes, you may." If he just says "Yes" and the player moves, the player must return to the starting line.

Fig. 10-23. Body warmup exercise. Courtesy NSPI.

Tip Top. The one who is "it" takes position in the middle of the pool. When he says "Go!" the players have to get into the water and swim to the other side. Any player caught by being touched on the head stays in the water and helps to catch the others. Last one caught wins.

Bolt Game. Here's a fun game that will help players learn to move underwater. The referee tosses several large bolts with nuts on them into waist-deep water. The players bend down, unscrew the nuts, and leave the bolts and nuts on the bottom. They straighten up, take deep breaths, and go under again to replace the nuts on the bolts under the water. The first to complete the tasks is the winner.

Balloon Volleyball. In this aquatic game, standard volleyball rules are followed. The problem is that players will find it tougher to get around in the water than in the gym. All you need is a net or rope stretched above the pool surface, a balloon, and at least two players. The more the merrier.

Ping-Pong Ball Race. Here's another "Egg and the Spoon" type race. In this case, the object is to blow the ping-pong ball ahead of you while you're swimming from one end of the pool to the other. You cannot touch it with your hands. The player who blows the ball across the pool first wins.

Sailboat Race. This game is similar to the Ping-Pong Ball Race just outlined, except that small sailboats must be blown across the pool. This is an excellent game for nonswimmers. If you don't have small plastic sailboats for this game, you can make them with flat boards and paper sails fastened to small wooden masts. Making them can be a fun winter project.

Fig. 10-24. The bigger the pool, the more fun available. Courtesy NSPI.

Bobbing for Corks. Players form lines on each side of the pool. The referee throws a handful of corks into the pool, then blows a whistle. Players jump in and the one collecting the greatest number of corks is the winner and new referee.

Red Light/Green Light. Here's a fun game for two or more players. The two individuals or groups face each other in the center of the pool about 5 feet apart. One side is "red" and the other is "green." The referee calls one of these colors. The color called tries to catch the others before they get back to their side of the pool.

MAKE UP YOUR OWN SWIMMING POOL GAMES

Aquatic games are both fun and useful as they teach swimming skills, sportsmanship, and teamwork. They are great for families and friends and can be easily adapted for different age groups.

One of the best ways of making up your own swimming pool games is to bring a number of swimmers together into a pool (Fig. 10-24). They will do the rest. The basic requirements of fun aquatic games include:

- ☐ Two or preferably more players
- ☐ An object (ball, cork, bolt, balloon, sailboat, inner tube, etc.)
- ☐ A location (center of the pool, sides of the pool, diving board, wading area, etc.)
- ☐ A goal (move the object, find the object, move from one location to another, etc.)
- ☐ A complication (competition, time, skill, etc.)

Dozens of games can be developed from these basic elements to make your swimming pool more enjoyable as swimming skills are developed. Most important, your swimming pool will be a safe place to swim and play.

Chapter 11

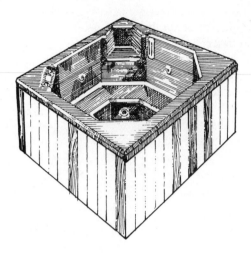

Hot Tubs And Spas

As the temperature soars or plunges, many people decide that the best escape is to create an aquatic world in their home by owning either a hot tub or spa (Fig. 11-1). For many, a hot tub or spa is a more practical addition than a swimming pool.

Installing a hot tub or spa in your backyard, on your patio, or inside your house doesn't necessarily require any major excavations or remodeling. It can be installed and ready to use within a couple of weeks.

Spas and hot tubs don't occupy much space, are relatively economical, and easy to maintain. The average hot tub, including all supporting equipment, costs between $2,500 and $4,000—about half that of a swimming pool. Spas start at $2,500 as well and increase in price with custom designs for special needs. Figure on another $1,000 to $2,000 for installation.

You can get the most from your hot tub or spa if you plan it carefully. Learn as much as you can about these pleasure baths in advance, then be a smart consumer as you make your selection.

HOT TUBS

A hot tub generally is round, straight-sided, about 4 feet deep and between 4 and 10 feet in diameter (Fig. 11-2). But it can also be oval or rectangular, have slanting sides, and be made of several kinds of wood, such as unstained redwood, cedar, cypress, mahogany, oak, or teak (Figs. 11-3 through 11-5). Hot tubs usually are equipped with electric water heaters, pumps, and filter to keep the water hot and clean. They also have hydrotherapy and multiple, adjustable, air-injection jets which warm, rapidly circulate, and filter the water.

Most hot tubs are assembled with beveled staves attached by metal hoops. Constant soaking keeps them watertight as water expands the wood to fill any cracks between the staves. Once a tub is installed, maintenance is somewhat more time-consuming than a spa's because wood is soft-textured, and more likely to deteriorate than other materials when not properly maintained.

Tubs have several advantages over spas. Above-grade installation makes them possible to move, al-

Fig. 11-1. Many people install hot tubs or spas as a practical addition to their swimming pool. Courtesy NSPI.

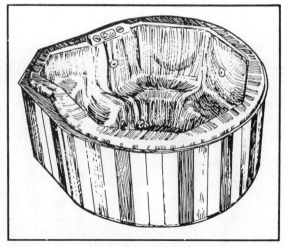

Fig. 11-3. Hot tubs come in all shapes. Courtesy Hytec, Inc.

though with some difficulty. From an energy standpoint, a wood hot tub is a better insulator than molded fiberglass, concrete, or Gunite. Finally, many prefer the hot tub made with natural wood which complements a rustic setting (Fig. 11-6).

SPAS

Spas are closely related to hot tubs (Fig. 11-7).

Both are pools of hot bubbling water. The difference is that while hot tubs are self-supporting wooden structures, spas usually are constructed of fiberglass or pneumatically-applied concrete.

Traditionally, spas have been located next to swimming pools and constructed of Gunite. Today, the majority of contemporary spas are molded from multiple layers of fiberglass coated with acrylic surface liner or gelcoat. This combination allows one-

Fig. 11-2. Typical hot tub.

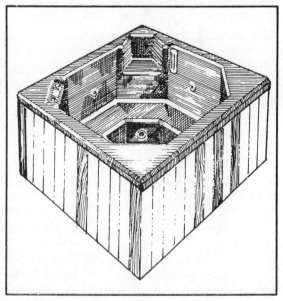

Fig. 11-4. Square hot tub. Courtesy Hytec, Inc.

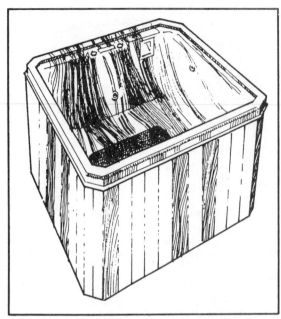

Fig. 11-5. Smaller square hot tub. Courtesy Hytec, Inc.

piece construction of an almost infinite array of sizes, shapes, and colors.

Although the shapes of spas are more variable than tubs, they follow the same basic pattern. Typically, they are 4 feet deep and 5 to 6 feet across, but they can also be somewhat smaller or larger. A few fiberglass spas are self-supporting and portable, but most must be excavated. Concrete spas, which are still primarily adjuncts to swimming pools, are durable and easy to maintain. Gunite spas provide the widest variety of shapes, but are the most costly. Fiberglass spas are generally easier to maintain than hot tubs or concrete and Gunite spas because the smooth, nonporous surface can be easily wiped clean.

Whirlpool spas, usually constructed of fiberglass-reinforced plastic, differ from baths in several ways. They are designed to be installed outdoors or inside (but separately from a regular bath or shower), are permanently filled with water, and must be frequently filtered and chlorinated.

If you live in a cold climate and want to move your spa indoors for the winter and outdoors for the summer, portable spas are the solution. Portable units, which have self-contained electrical, heating,

filtration, and pump equipment, are gaining popularity. They're also ideal for people who rent or move frequently.

If you can't decide between a hot tub or spa, it's now possible to get the best of both worlds. A recent innovation in hot tubs is the spa-tub which, like the portable spas, can be used and moved indoors and outdoors. This hybrid unit is a wooden tub with a smooth vinyl liner. It meshes the beauty of a hot tub with the clean lines of a fiberglass spa. Besides being easier to clean, its insulation prevents heat loss, provides a cushioned interior, and doesn't leak.

HOW TO SHOP FOR QUALITY

When you shop for a spa or tub, you'll find that many units appear identical. Judging a model based on its appearance is dangerous. Know what to look for in good quality materials, workmanship, and design to insure that you get both what you want and what you pay for.

Here's a good checklist for buying a hot tub (Figs. 11-8 to 11-11), offered by the National Spa and Pool Institute:

- ☐ Look for tight, vertical-grain lumber without defects such as knots, decay, splits, or milling imperfections.
- ☐ Sides, bottom, and seats should be constructed of the same quality heartwood, which is the darker colored wood cut from the center of the tree. Heartwood resists decay and is more durable than the lighter colored sapwood.
- ☐ Joints should be tight with no interior

Fig. 11-6. A hot tub can add value to your home. Courtesy NSPI.

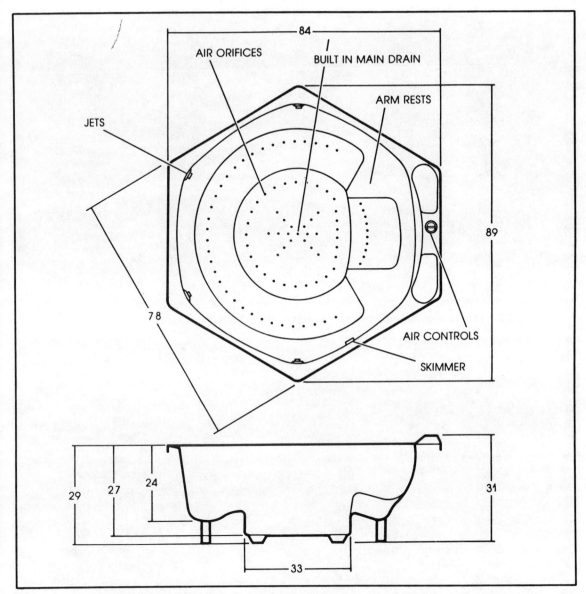

Fig. 11-7. Spas are built-in hot tubs. Courtesy Baja Industries, Inc.

crevices where bacteria and algae can grow.

☐ Staves should be at least 1 5/8 inches thick as the tub will last longer and retain heat better. Grooves in the staves that secure the floorboards should be milled so staves come in full contact with the floorboards.

☐ Edges around the floorboards should be routed or precision-cut to reduce splinter-ing. The floorboards should be routed and sanded smooth to prevent splitting and re-duce splintering.

☐ Bands or hoops should be rustproof and have capped protrusions to prevent ac-cidents.

☐ Benches should not interfere with cleaning the tub floor or with water circulation.

Fig. 11-8. Typical hot tub outdoor installation. Courtesy Western Wood Products Assn.

Fig. 11-9. A hot tub should have greater privacy than a pool. Courtesy Western Wood Products Assn.

Fig. 11-10. A hot tub can be used for entertaining. Courtesy Western Wood Products Assn.

SHOPPING FOR SPAS

Quality in fiberglass spas is harder to pinpoint than in tubs. Neither design or shape is an indicator. The surest test is to rely on the manufacturer's reputation for producing a quality product. The points to check:

☐ Consistent thickness along the edges and absence of cracks or creases anywhere
☐ Well-made molds with visible reinforcement at the steps, across the bottom, and around all outlets
☐ An interior lining that is blemish free and with no scratches or pockmarks
☐ A shell exterior with reinforcing ribs around the seats and plumbing outlets
☐ Smoothness of the tile work

Most experts agree that either gelcoat or acrylic linings are suitable for spas. Gelcoat, a colored polyester-resin, has been applied over molded-fiberglass products like pools, spas, and boats for years. It is slightly less expensive than acrylic but more susceptible to the ultraviolet and infrared rays of the sun and chemicals, so it requires more routine maintenance and has a duller appearance. Acrylic is more resistant to abrasion and can withstand chemical damage and higher temperature.

THE FRINGE BENEFITS

A good soak in hot water can tone and relax your muscles, relieve anxiety and nervous tension, increase blood circulation, and generally make you feel a lot better. It could even save you some medical bills associated with arthritis, back pains, painful joints, ulcers, and other stress-related health problems

Beside their medicinal and recreational benefits, hot tubs and spas may qualify for tax credits if needed for theraputic reasons and

155

prescribed by your physician. Anyone planning to claim a medical deduction should seek advice from a tax specialist. The cost can only be deducted to the extent it exceeds the value the improvement adds to a property. So, if a spa installation costs $6,000, but adds only $4,000 to the property value, the capital deduction can only be $2,000.

Should you sell your property, the cost of a tub or spa can be deducted from your profits on the sale, thereby reducing your capital gains.

OPTIONS

Options and accessories that can be purchased range from the practical—hand skimmers to remove debris, bubble systems, thermometers, covers, and water treatment kits—to the fanciful—remote switches, outdoor showers, tub scents, and toys (Figs. 11-12 through 11-15).

You'll need support equipment to heat, circulate, and filter water in your spa or hot tub. Remember these points as you shop for them:

- ☐ Make sure the heater is the right size. It should be large enough to heat the water quickly and maintain the desired temperature, but small enough to be energy-efficient.
- ☐ Be sure your pump is the proper size for your system. Plastic pumps, the most widely used, vary in durability and price. Con-

Fig. 11-11. A hot tub should be located near the showers. Courtesy Western Wood Products Assn.

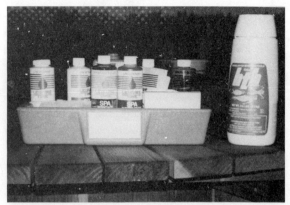

Fig. 11-12. You should have your water chemical maintenance tray located near your hot tub or spa.

As an unsecured home improvement loan, no collateral is required. The term of the loan is usually from five to seven years. Larger loans with longer payback periods are available if you decide to secure the loan.

A variety of other options are available including home equity loans, which permit you to refinance your house and leave you with excess cash to use. Or you can take out a second mortgage as a high-interest, short-term loan. Check with banks on what approach is best for you. But remember that by refinancing an older mortgage, you may be subject to today's higher interest rates—a situation that could cost you thousands of dollars in interest.

sider purchasing a 24-hour timer which automatically runs your filtration pump.
☐ Selecting the right pipes and fitting is also important.

FINANCING

If you're hesitating to purchase a spa or hot tub because of the cost, you may wish to consider the several ways of financing your purchase. Home improvement loans are the most common method and are available from banks, savings and loan associations, and some credit unions.

BEFORE YOU BUY

Now that you know the basics, where do you go? Find out which dealers in your area have the best selection of spas by asking friends and neighbors and by checking the Yellow Pages. Members of professional and industrial associations, such as the NSPI, subscribe to strict standards for proper manufacturing and installation and stand behind their products.

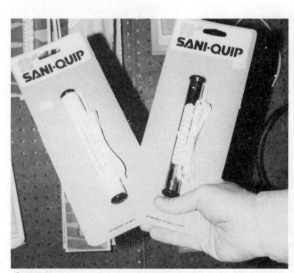

Fig. 11-13. Hot tub thermometers are available in many styles.

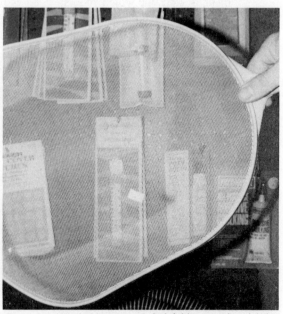

Fig. 11-14. Hand skimmers are helpful in removing debris.

157

Fig. 11-15. Outdoor shower unit.

Also, follow these tips as they are your best assurance against legal and financial headaches in buying your hot tub or spa:

☐ When shopping for a spa or tub, call companies that repair and service the equipment to find out which models need the fewest repairs. Find out the terms of warranties offered by various manufacturers, what's covered and what isn't, how long the warranty is in effect, and other considerations.

☐ Avoid dealers, installers, and builders who won't put everything in writing. You should know when the work will start and be completed, financing arrangements, and total costs for labor and all materials.

☐ Look for dealers who will supply references of satisfied customers. Call the Better Business Bureau and your local consumer affairs agency to see whether any customers have lodged complaints against the dealer.

☐ Ask the dealer and contractor for credit references to make sure they are financially solvent and can stand behind their promises. "Fad" businesses have a high mortality rate and may not be in business

to back up guarantees a year from now.

☐ In states where licensing is required, check with the State Contractor Licensing Board to be certain the installing contractor is licensed, bonded, and insured for worker's compensation. Otherwise, the injury of a workman on your premises could be your financial responsibility. Any licensed dealer or installer can give you the telephone number of the state contractor's board.

INSTALLING YOUR HOT TUB OR SPA

There's nothing new about the pleasures and therapeutic benefits of soaking in a tub of soothing, hot water. For centuries the Romans, Greeks, Egyptians, Turks, and Japaneses used hot baths to cleanse their bodies and to relax and commune with friends and family.

Today, hot tubs and spas are again heating up for a growing legion of aficianados from coast to coast. In a matter of weeks you can convert a square room, backyard, or an unoccupied nook into your own Garden of Eden. The secret is choosing and blending design elements to achieve the desired effect. Let's consider some of the design elements important to installing your own hot tub or spa.

Mild climates make it easy to install a spa or tub outside, but living in a cold climate won't limit your options. Any number of locations indoors or out can be used to create a year-round setting for your hot tub or spa:

☐ A glass porch enclosure makes an ideal greenhouse for plants while it helps to heat the water and air around the spa.

☐ A screened-in patio with sliding glass doors does double-duty as an enclosed structure in the winter that opens up in the summer (Figs. 11-16 to 11-19).

☐ An air-inflated plastic enclosure covers the spa or tub for winter bathing and comes off in warm weather.

Another option is to install a portable spa or hot tub which can be moved indoors during cold weather, as mentioned earlier. All that's required to in-

Fig. 11-16. Indoor hot tub. Courtesy Western Wood Products Assn.

stall most portable spas is an acceptable location and an electrical outlet. During warmer months, place your spa or hot tub inside a latticed gazebo, or make it the focal point in a narrow or small garden using plant materials and decking for contrasting effect.

FINDING SPACE

Sometimes considered an obstacle, a challenging landscape can actually work in your favor. One bonus of a steep hillside is that it becomes the home of a multilevel deck off the master bedroom with a sweeping view of the valley and mountains and a secluded spa. The owners get the best of two worlds: a spa close to the house that capitalizes on their property's grand view.

One of the biggest obstacles to overcome in designing hillside spas or hot tubs is finding room for sunbathing, relaxing, and other outdoor activities. A hillside deck in the front of the house, off to the side, or in back is the simplest solution. Another way is to excavate a level spot in the hillside. Retaining walls are used to terrace the lot into separate levels, and planting areas help delineate various areas.

Another way to make space is to literally carve a spa out of a hillside. Walls and ceilings can be formed with reinforced concrete, and natural rock pillars at the entrance will make you think you're soaking in a grotto. If rock is impractical, use precast, textured concrete to achieve the same effect.

The absence of trees and other foliage which provide shade need not be a deterrent to creating a pleasing ambience. An overhead structure like an open-sided gazebo or vertical screen or circular openings provides shade and filters sunlight without blocking the view.

If you already own a pool or are contemplating a pool purchase, consider the popular outdoor spa and pool combination which is ideal for warmer climates. Install a hot tub or spa in a forest-like setting at the end of your pool or directly beside it and you can take an invigorating swim, then relax and soak in the bubbly hot water of your spa or tub. A concrete dam could be used to separate the spa area from the main pool, or the spa shape could be designed to swerve around the line of curved steps leading to a free-form pool.

Don't forget the landscaping around the spa/hot tub site. Outdoor entertainment deck or patio areas, complete with contrasting tile, boulders, brick, or wood, complement the spa and hot tub, as do selective plantings. Wood, flagstone, creek stones, or exposed aggregate walking surfaces create the more natural settings. Tile, masonry, or textured concrete lend themselves more to formality. Consider designing the landscape in the theme of an Aztec hideaway using warm earth tones of brick and adobe, or as a California garden with warm, natural wood tones set against a backdrop of bamboo and ferns.

Indoor space for a spa can be made by adding or remodeling a bedroom, den, or living room. The room can be transformed into an exercise center

Fig. 11-17. Patio door can open a hot tub to the outside world in warmer weather. Courtesy Western Wood Products Assn.

Fig. 11-18. A patio hot tub can be easily heated during colder months. Courtesy Western Wood Products Assn.

Fig. 11-19. A shower can be easily installed nearby. Courtesy Western Wood Products Assn.

complete with weight-lifting equipment, tanning machine, and if space permits, a sauna. The latest innovation is the "wetroom."

INSTALLING A WETROOM

Primarily a European phenomenon, wetrooms are new to this side of the Atlantic. A well-stocked wetroom is a home fitness center (Fig. 11-20). It can include an eight-person oblong octagonal spa, a six-person steam room, a shower stall/dressing area, an isolated/relaxation tank—in which a person floats in warm, salinated water devoid of light and sound—an ultraviolet tanning bench, and exercise equipment.

Other products that could be incorporated into a wetroom include a jetted tub—a bathtub fitted with spa jets—or a controlled environment room that accommodates two people and operates as a sauna, steam room, shower, or tanning room. Some of these unique rooms also come equipped with adjustable lighting, stereophonic sound, and video screens.

HOT TUB AND SPA SAFETY

To get the maximum benefit and enjoyment out

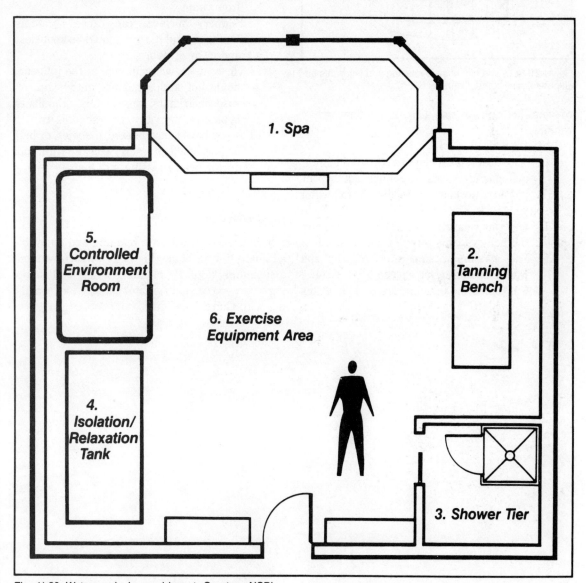

1. Spa

5. Controlled Environment Room

2. Tanning Bench

6. Exercise Equipment Area

4. Isolation/ Relaxation Tank

3. Shower Tier

Fig. 11-20. Wetroom design and layout. Courtesy NSPI.

Fig. 11-21. Spas and hot tubs are relaxing and enjoyable additions to your home. Courtesy NSPI.

of your hot tub or spa, here are a few safety reminders:

☐ Since heat relaxes muscles beyond their normal pliancy, avoid strenuous activity or physical workouts immediately following your soak. The benefits of a hot soak lie in fostering relaxation, as well as in releasing the body's toxins through perspiration.

☐ The maximum temperature of the spa waters should never exceed 104° F. (40° C.). Check the temperature of your water *before* getting in.

☐ Avoid long exposures. To get the maximum physical pleasure from your spa, begin a routine in which you observe a reasonable time limit (no more than 15 minutes), leave the spa, then shower, cool down, and if you wish, return for another brief stay.

☐ For the sake of comfort and safety, persons with long hair should tie their hair in a bun or knot to keep it out of the water and away from drains.

☐ Slippery surfaces can cause accidents. Decks around the spa should be kept clean and clear of debris.

☐ Never use a spa while under the influence of alcohol, anticoagulants, antihistamines, vasoconstrictors, vasodilators, stimulants, hypnotics, narcotics, or tranquilizers.

☐ If you have heart disease, diabetes, or high or low blood pressure, consult with your doctor before getting into a spa.

SUMMING UP

Spas and hot tubs are relaxing and enjoyable additions to your home (Fig.11-21), with or without a swimming pool. By planning wisely and shopping smart you can gain greater satisfaction from living with God's great gift: water

Glossary

algae—Microscopic plant growth found in all bodies of water. Whenever conditions are unfavorable to their growth, they dry up into spores and float upon the wind until carried to a puddle, pond, stream, or pool. The air is almost always full of countless millions of algae spores, especially during hot weather. When algae are introduced into chemically untreated swimming pool water, they thrive and multiply rapidly. Crystal clear water soon turns a solid green color. Not only do algae cause the water to appear unsightly, they can also cause serious water pollution. They can be reduced or eliminated in swimming pool water through the use of algaecides.

alum—An acid salt for floccing or settling to the pool floor matter suspended throughout the pool water.

backwash piping—The piping which extends from the backwash outlet of the filters to its terminus at the point of disposal.

chemical residual—That concentration at which a chemical must be maintained in solution in the swimming pool so that the chemical can do its work effectively.

chlorine—A germicide used for residential swimming pools.

diatomaceous earth (diatomite)—Minute, variously shaped, silica skeletons of diatoms which were small, single-cell marine plants that lived ages ago. Diatomaceous earth is often used as a filter medium in swimming pool filters.

facepiping—The piping that connects the vacuum fitting to the pump suction.

fill-and-draw pool—A pool which has no provision for recirculating and filtering the pool water, such as a wading pool.

filter—Any material or apparatus by which water is clarified.

filter element—That part of a filter device which removes the suspended particles from the water.

filter media—The fine material at the surface of the filter element which entraps the suspended particles.

filter pool—A pool having a recirculating filter system. The water in a filter pool is maintained at consistently high standards of clarity and purity with much less vacuuming and cleaning, and at a lower chemical-treatment cost than is the water in a fill-and-draw pool.

filter rock—Graded rock and gravel used to support filter sand.

filter sand—A type of filter medium.

floccing—Floccing swimming pool water consists

of adding a chemical to the water (usually alum) for the purpose of settling suspended dirt or any other solids to the pool floor.

flow-through pool—A pool having a continuous flow of water into and out of the pool. Usually the water source is a spring or stream.

inlet—The fitting or opening through which water enters the pool.

main outlet—The outlet(s) at the deep portion of the pool through which the main flow of water leaves the pool.

main suction—The line connecting the main outlet to the pump suction.

make-up water—Fresh, chemically untreated water which is periodically added to pools to make up for evaporation, leakage, or other losses.

overflow gutter—A trough in the wall of the pool which may be used as an overflow and to skim the pool surface.

pH—A chemical symbol denoting the degree of alkalinity or acidity of pool water.

pH-plus blocks—These are fused cakes of sodium carbonate (soda ash) used to counteract acidity in pool water and to restore pH to the alkaline side.

pH scale—The range of alkalinity or acidity of a solution. The pH scale ranges from 0.0 to 14.0. The neutral point on the scale is 7.0. In testing the pool water, any reading below 7.0 indicates the water is on the acid side. Any reading above 7.0 indicates the water is on the alkaline side.

pool deck—The surface area around the pool.

pool depths—The distance between the floor of the pool and maximum operating level.

pool pH range—For effective operation of many pool water-treatment chemicals, the pH of the water should range from neutral (7.0) to slightly alkaline (7.6). In certain sections of the country, particularly the West, slightly higher pH values have been found better for efficient pool operation. The pH of the water is continuously affected by many factors: bathing load, certain water treatment chemicals, etc. The pH should be checked frequently with a water testing kit. When the pH of the water is out of the desirable range, it should be treated promptly with the proper chemicals to bring it into balance again.

receptor—An approved plumbing fixture or device of such material, shape, and capacity as to adequately receive the discharge from indirect waste piping, so constructed and located as to be readily cleaned.

recirculating piping—The piping from the pool to the filter and return to the pool through which the water circulates.

recirculating skimmer—A device connected with the pump suction used to skim the pool over a self-adjusting weir and return the water to the pool through the filter.

residential swimming pool—Any constructed pool which is used or intended to be used as a swimming pool in connection with a single family residence and available only to the family of the householder and his private guests.

return piping—The piping which carries the filtered water from the filter to the pool.

sodium bisulphite—An acid salt used to counteract excess alkalinity in pool water.

swimming pool—Any constructed pool, used for swimming or bathing, over 24 inches in depth, or with a surface area exceeding 250 square feet.

underdrain—An appurtenance at the bottom of the filter to assure equal distribution of water through the filter media.

vacuum fitting—The fitting in the wall of the pool which is used as a convenient outlet for connecting the underwater suction cleaning equipment.

vacuum piping—The piping which connects the vacuum fitting to the pump suction.

water testing kit—The necessary equipment for determining (1) the chlorine residual or amount of chlorine in the pool, and (2) the pH or degree of alkalinity or acidity of the water.

Index